THE BEST DAMN TRUMPET PLAYER

MEMORIES OF THE BIG BAND ERA AND BEYOND

by

RICHARD GRUDENS

CELEBRITY PROFILES PUBLISHING
Stony Brook, N.Y. 11790

PHOTOS BY
C. CAMILLE SMITH AND GUS YOUNG

Library of Congress
Catalog Card Number 96-83106

ISBN 1-57579-011-4

Published by:
Celebrity Profiles
Box 344, Main Street
Stony Brook, New York 11790-0344
(516) 862-8555

Edited by MaryLou Facciolo

Printed in United States of America

PINE HILL PRESS, INC.
Freeman, S. Dak. 57029

Table of Contents

iii

iv

Foreword

by Frankie Laine

Starting with the Big Bands in the 1930's and continuing through today, we've been blessed with the opportunity to enjoy music that creates a feeling of well being and familiarity. Not the frenetic sounds of the various types of rock, but the pure melodic sounds of some bands and the swinging jazz styles of others have provided a common bond between all peoples, no matter what their nationalities or social backgrounds.

Time, unfortunately, has robbed us of the pleasure of having most of the early "greats" among us physically, but their recordings survive them. One can't help but wonder how, for instance, Glenn Miller's style would have evolved over the years had he not met his untimely death.

The Big Bands served a purpose aside from soothing our senses with their musical arrangements—they spawned such legendary singers as Doris Day, Kay Starr, and Frank Sinatra, to name a few. Although severely restricted in the development of their own styles while with bands, many band singers eventually went out on their own, giving them the opportunity to be as innovative as their capabilities permitted.

The sensational Nat "King" Cole was one of the first balladeers to start his career without the aid of a Big Band background. He and his trio plugged along until fame simply had to follow. And, not to "blow my own horn," but I believe I was the first white male singer to achieve success sans a Big Band boost. Definitely not an easy road, but I've never regretted any of the hardship, as I met many kind, helpful people on the way up. Among them were Perry Como, Carl Fischer, Al Jolson, Hoagy Carmichael and Al Jarvis.

There are still great musical groups and singers which have emerged even in the 80's and 90's. Harry Connick, Jr. is a "throwback" to the "good old days": Barbra Streisand and Whitney Houston are two of the greatest female singers ever, and Natalie Cole is a credit to her father's memory.

Richard Grudens embarked on a labor of love, painstakingly researching the lives of many of the greats of the past several decades. Some of these musicians are or were personal friends. Over the past months, I have looked forward to receiving the book in installments as he wrote it, and I know you will share my enthusiasm and pleasure as you read the anecdotes and facts about some of our best loved performers.

But come—spend a few hours reminiscing about the people who will live in our hearts and, hopefully, our children's, forever.

Frankie Laine
San Diego, California
April 1996

Preface

Every boy has his heroes. For some, it's the crew of *StarTrek* and the *Enterprise*. Others may find the complex imagination of Thomas Edison or Albert Einstein spellbinding. I have friends, as you may, who revere the demeanor of a John Wayne movie or the bat and speed of Mickey Mantle. My heroes were the bandleaders and vocalists of the thirties, forties, and fifties, in a time known as *The Big Band Era*. The art of its many participants meant countless hours of musical and vocal delight to me and to millions the world over.

Here you could find, as my mother once defined for me, the noisy, brash sounds she didn't necessarily appreciate because it eclipsed her own heroes, those sturdy Sigmund Romberg operettas, and her favorite Jeanette McDonald and Nelson Eddy duets, as well as her love for the very early Russ Columbo and Bing Crosby recordings. All this was, of course, the beginning of what was to come.

The Big Bands did for me what I'm certain Elvis Presley or John Lennon did for others. They served up that needed musical nourishment. When I skipped downtown Manhattan high school classes in the late forties, I traded math and English for the sights and sounds of Benny Goodman, Harry James, Count Basie, Glenn Miller, Woody Herman, Vaughan Monroe, or Gene Krupa at the Paramount, the Strand, or the Roxy theaters. I was a New York kid listening to the sounds of my time helped considerably by New York's radio station, WNEW and its legendary disk jockey, Martin Block.

Many years passed, and then suddenly and urgently in 1980, I realized my heroes were disappearing from the face of the earth: No, no, not their music, individual or collective, which, of course, is permanently preserved on records, tapes, and C.D.s, but the living man and woman, the flesh and blood human who actually performed this music for my own personal pleasure, providing me with that musical nutrition. So I realized then I had to meet with them face-to-face, elbow-to-elbow, eyeball-to-eyeball, hand-to-hand before it was too late and they were all gone. Celebrity Profiles, a small company organized to manage and represent me, was formed and a search for those heroes began.

Fortunately for me, a freelance writer and former NBC Newswriter, I inadvertently ran across a small tabloid-size entertainment-oriented newspaper called *Long Island PM* which was circulated through Long Island restaurants and entertainment centers and owned and operated by Paul Raymond of Central Islip, who had previously published *Spotlight Magazine.*

In one particular issue, Paul advertised for writers, and I answered the call submitting a query for a short article about an interesting and little known (but much revered) Big Band arranger, Bill Challis, who was part of Paul Whiteman's great King Of Jazz Orchestra and who once arranged for legendary cornetist, Bix Biederbecke, and bandleaders Jean Goldkette and Glenn Miller, to name a few. Bill and I shared many hours together discussing big band material when he worked as a dispatcher in a cement-block yard in Uniondale and I was a traveling salesman for a building material wholesaler during the late 1960's.

Raymond accepted the piece, and I was on my way. The first assignment was an interview with Broadway's Earl Wrightson and Lois Hunt at their home in nearby Brookville. The results were good, and although he could not pay me much, we hit it off and I traded my acceptance as his chief entertainment writer for expenses, but I didn't care since it was a jumpstart towards my goal.

The rest of the story is contained on these pages. My appreciation goes out to Paul Raymond, for his little paper was the catalyst for the implementation of my otherwise impossible dream. And a special thanks goes to my friend, mentor and advisor, Frankie Laine, for encouragement and special help along the way and to my wife and companion of 27 years, Jeanette for her patience and participation in this adventure.

RICHARD GRUDENS, STONYBROOK, NEW YORK 1996

Glenn Miller Band, circa 1939, Photo credit: Ed Burke collection.

Tommy Dorsey Band 1938. Buddy Rich on drums, rear row: Pied Pipers on left with Jo Stafford; Connie Haines next to Young Frank Sinatra, Johnny Mince second from left (front row). Photo credit: Ed Burke collection.

The Big Bands
Will They Ever Return?

The Perennial Plight of Big Band Fans

It was Thomas Wolfe who wisely counseled the romantics when he declared, "You can never go home again," but some people are afflicted with what is known as Joe DiMaggio Syndrome, where they fantasize that someday the legendary Yankee Clipper will return to Yankee Stadium once again to smash a home run that will win a close pennant- race. Similarly, there are those who once believed that someday entertainers Dean Martin & Jerry Lewis would be reunited as a television team to repeat those great comedy routines, and some followers of the Ian Fleming 007 spy thriller movies may just expect Sean Connery to suddenly rejuvenate his body and make over his face to personally embark on yet another James Bond film to please the faithful millions.

Despite all this fantasy, some people still speculate about the return of the Big Bands. But it will never take place. It would never work. After bandleader Glenn Miller's Air Force plane disappeared over the English Channel that foggy December night in 1944, a number of valiant attempts to revive the band were tried by former band members Jerry Gray and Ray Anthony, and later, Tex Beneke, Ray McKinley, Ralph Flanagan and Buddy DeFranco, in order to keep the "Miller sound" (clarinet lead on the saxophone section) alive for its millions of fans. Although they met with varying degrees of success, they were unable to fully re-create the original elusive, disciplined sound that Glenn worked for so long and so hard before he reached his extraordinary success. (It was Woody Herman who told me the little-known fact that both Glenn and his wife Helen's parents had to obtain second mortgages on their homes in order to keep the band going.) Glenn's stern dedication, and all-around talent for keeping the

1

band together was no longer present, nor was his skillful editing and unique choice of arrangers and their arrangements—the leader, after all, was gone; the successors did not last—the genuine intonations could easily be distinguished from any creative substitutions. And Woody further noted, "that if Glenn were alive today, he would be probably playing something different." Woody, although proud of his past, played only the music of the current day—his interpretations, of course, and survived with a youthful group well into the eighties when I first became acquainted with him:

"If I had to keep playing the same old stuff I played 40 years ago it would be boring—I'd have thrown in the towel a long time ago."

Of course, Glenn Miller became an icon due to an early death (much the same as Elvis Presley) which occurred during the height of his career. However, his music is still played today. The Glenn Miller Band, to this date controlled by the Miller family and directed by Larry O'Brien, plays almost every day somewhere in the U.S. or elsewhere, but mostly its original charts.

During the 1920's and 1930's the foundation of the Big Band Era was set in place by its many participants. It was officially launched, however, one eventful evening in 1935 at the Palomar Ballroom in Los Angeles by the Benny Goodman band who was tired of playing the expected dance charts and defiantly broke out into a wild, swinging session which surprised and delighted everyone. The crowd just went wild and the King of Swing was crowned that night. The Big Band era developed and cured slowly as one band after another was spawned in a process where individual band members spun off successive bands to form their own musical organizations. The immensely popular Paul Whiteman, Fletcher Henderson, and Ben Pollack bands alone accounted for many spin-offs: Louis Armstrong and Coleman Hawkins spun off Henderson; Benny Goodman, Glenn Miller, Charlie Spivack, and Jack Teagarden off Pollack; Tommy and Jimmy Dorsey (and many players like Bix Beiderbecke and Joe Venuti—and singers like Bing Crosby and Mildred Bailey) off Whiteman.

It was an uphill fight for those pioneers: "We were all struggling," said Harry James in his last interview with me in 1984, "and nobody was getting paid. Guys were jumping from one band to another. I almost gave up (running my own band) a number of times."

2

So this was proof enough they were traveling in an uncertain direction, wondering if the band itself would even survive a few weeks or months as it criss-crossed the circuit set by the booking agencies. But in retrospect, the Big Bands and their participants caught on and persisted until the brash loudness of a new era drowned them out and helped lower them into a nostalgic graveyard, but only after some twenty years of phenomenal success, hundreds of Hollywood movies, and ten times ten-thousand remote broadcasts and recordings.

Conditions in the late thirties were right for the formation of the Big Bands. There were dance pavilions, ballrooms, and large moviehouse stages where big bands could play to standing room only audiences. Big Band leaders and their vocalists became the great celebrities of the day, and each band usually had a vocal group like the Pied Pipers, Modernaires, King Sisters, or the Andrews Sisters, wherein some of the later vocalists developed their craft.

The Big Bands and their leaders dominated most prime-time network radio whether on their own or as a feature attraction on big-time shows. Skinnay Ennis on Bob Hope, John Scott Trotter on Bing Crosby, Billy Mills on Fibber-Magee & Molly, and Phil Harris on Jack Benny. Benny Goodman, Glenn Miller, The Dorsey Brothers, and Ozzie Nelson, were radio regulars with their own programs. With network radio linking stations from New York to California, the shows could be heard coast-to-coast for the first time, the bands often performing live from large hotels, great ballrooms, and endless radio studios throughout the land.

After the war, for many reasons, the very popular dance pavilions began closing. Most were located in amusement parks in just about the outskirts of every town which were accessible by electric trolleys or surface railroads After the war, automobiles and airplanes radically changed the way people lived and traveled so they were no longer restricted to simply attending Big Band dances at nearby, convenient town pavilions. It was also a time when street railways were being dismantled in favor of the more mobile buses and automobiles, overwhelmingly promoted by expanding oil and tire companies, now back in post-war consumer production. Automobiles could transport you to the drive-in movie, where couples had more privacy, or down newly

3

constructed interstates or freeways leading to attractions practically anywhere.

Then came the advent of television which kept Big Band fans at home. The Big Band radio showcases diminished in favor of the new programs flickering across the revolutionary picture tube located in the center of their own living rooms. Some large movie theaters shut down. Remote broadcasts were silenced. Network radio was forced to reduce its excellent array of musical programs for lack of listeners. Wrestling matches and roller derbys prevailed. *Howdy Doody, I Love Lucy, Studio One,* and *Ed Sullivan* replaced Benny Goodman and Artie Shaw. All these changes contributed to the demise of the beautifully developed musical wonder we knew as The Big Band Era, giving way to an age of the great vocalists: Frank Sinatra, Frankie Laine, Dick Haymes, Perry Como, Kay Starr, Margaret Whiting, Doris Day, Billy Eckstine, Sarah Vaughan, Dinah Shore, Patti Page, Rosemary Clooney, and dozens of others, mostly on recordings, then graduating to the television tube itself, although some of them started with those Big Bands. Eventually, the encroachment of rock and roll and Top Forty radio pressed forward with The Beatles and Elvis Presley leading the charge, which has surprisingly lasted over thirty years.

So the Big Band Era was composed of special ingredients like those occurring in a classic painting—never to be captured again in quite the same way. Will there ever be another Glenn Miller, Tommy Dorsey, or Benny Goodman? Will there ever be another Renoir or Picasso? The will and interest to exactly recreate any success is one of man's eternal failings. The manner in which a successful creation evolves can never be planned or measured in advance.

I doubt that anyone during this period could have simply created the Big Band phenomenon by declaring: "Let's organize Benny, Glenn, Erskine, Duke, Harry and the rest of the musicians on this list and get them started in their own bands and we'll call it the *Big Band Era.* It would never have worked. After all, even though these men, with the help of their sidemen, arrangers, songwriters, and the girl, boy and group singers, instituted and dominated the performance of almost all popular music for some 25 years, it is certain that it evolved quite accidentally. Today dedicated followers try over and over again to proclaim a rebirth of the Big Bands, but who will perform the melodious *Frenesi* with the undulating excellence that was once the fastidious clarinet of Artie Shaw, or dish up the brassy, expressive trumpet of Harry James on *You Made Me Love You?* Nor would we want them to; nor would we really expect them to. And who will you find to replace Glenn Miller performing his little masterpiece, *Moonlight Serenade*? Who would play *Apple Honey*? or *Caledonia*?...surely not even Woody himself. "My favorite record is the one we'll make next year!" Woody once declared to me, "You can't live in the past."

Further proof would be that none of the above selections from those bygone days could ever sound the same musically or spiritually. You would need the original players in their corresponding frame of mind and musical form. You would require the same quality studio, mikes, instruments and equipment, good or bad. The chemical expression and ability of each of those players would have to be identical. Any attempt or change of any ingredient would simply be something new and different. As Agatha Christie once said about a character in one of her stories, the Big Band revival fan is an "old soldier with an unfortunate weakness for reliving the past."

It has been said that music constantly changes. "Music today is completely different than the music of the forties." Harry James explained, "You would think that people would like only the old stuff. Not so. Anyway, I don't think you can compare what you used to do with what you have to do to stay alive in this business today."

The Big Band Era is considered history now, with the usual, lingering after-shocks, including revival, reliving, reunion and, of course, the written word. Along the Big Band circuit you can presently find many "ghost" bands, a phrase coined by Woody Herman, where big jazz or dance bands operate without the leaders for whom they are named. Basie, Miller, Shaw, Ellington, Kay Kyser, Harry James, Guy Lombardo, Buddy Rich and other "ghost" bands regularly tour with new members and ever-changing leaders. Today, Frank Foster directs the Basie Band; The Duke's son, Mercer, has led the Ellington Band since 1974 after his father passed on; Shaw sometimes directs his band from the wings. Trombonist Buddy Morrow leads the Tommy Dorsey Band; Lee Castle, former sideman, directs the Jimmy

Dorsey Orchestra, and Frank Tiberi, a veteran of the Woody Herman band, leads the newest Thundering Herd.

In his book *The Big Bands,* longtime critic and companion to many of the players, George Simon, had this to say: "I doubt whether any other group of artists has ever managed to develop and produce so consistently well under such trying conditions as did the musicians in the Big Bands. Obviously they were all part of something more inspiring than mere materialism. They shared what too few working groups share; a love of what they were doing, a love coupled with a healthy conviction that they were both playing and fighting for a cause to which they were deeply dedicated."

The Big Bands were the delicious musical relics of the past who attached their indelible mark upon several generations of music lovers—both those who liked to dance and those who preferred to listen. Through the modern magic of magnetic tape and compact disks with their advanced technology, the excellence of the Big Band Era carries on. It will never "come back" for it has been clearly over for some time and I don't think you'll see the likes of it ever again. This book will offer to chronicle a portion of the lives of some of the principal participants in and successors to the Big Band Era.

1940's Harry James Band. Photo credit: Ed Burke collection.

Harry James leads the band while Helen Forrest sings.
Photo credit: Big Band Jump.

Harry Haag James
Plays His Horn

Most people seem to remember Harry James and his band more from appearances in those splashy, glitzy 1940's movies, *Springtime in the Rockies* and *Best Foot Forward,* and the fact that he was married to World War II's most popular pinup, Betty Grable, *the girl with the world's most beautiful legs,* who also starred in those films. The couple would appear together on the covers of ubiquitous fan magazines.

"Where's Betty?" some rude fans would shout to him on the streets of Hollywood and New York. They forgot that a few years earlier, he was a very youthful, vibrant and stellar trumpet playing bandleader of the Big Band Era and the man who holds the unique distinction of discovering an unknown young singer by the name of Frank Sinatra.

"So it's true!" I was talking with Harry James in his dressing room in 1981 at Northport High School on Long Island's North Shore just prior to his appearance on stage with his band.

"Well, you know Frank! He wouldn't say it if it wasn't."

"So tell me how it all happened." I really wanted to hear this first hand account because over the years I had heard so many versions.

"I was at the Brooklyn Paramount when I first started, and he was playing at a little place called the Rustic Cabin near Alpine, New Jersey, and I used to hear him on a local radio show from there when I was coming home, and I didn't know who he was because they didn't say. We needed a vocalist for our new band, so the next day I found out where he was, and I went to talk to him, and he wound up joining the band." Frank was actually the Master of Ceremonies, headwaiter, and sometime singer for the Rustic Cabin.

"But I heard he left you before his contract was up."

9

"Sure, because we were all starving and his wife was pregnant (with Nancy) and she was going to have that baby any minute and he had a chance to go with Tommy Dorsey for $120.00 a week. He was only making $75.00 with me and not getting it because we were struggling. So I gave him my blessing and said if things don't get better with us in the next six months, get me a job with Dorsey."(They got better, of course, and Dick Haymes replaced Sinatra.)

Harry's agent, Willard Alexander, told me he thought Harry James was one of the most powerful performers in the band business. "He was always musically in charge. His trumpet poured out the strains of his music, and it made weak songs strong." Willard headed the New York booking agency that bore his name and was mentor and agent to many Big Band leaders for many years. It was Alexander and impresario, Sol Hurok who presumptuously organized the landmark 1939 Benny Goodman Concert at Carnegie Hall that featured Harry on the trumpet playing in his first major jazz concert. He was in his best possible form. He sparked the other players. His playing knew no bounds that night, being self-assured, controlled, and just about technically perfect.

Harry Haag James was born on March 15, 1916 in Albany, Georgia. He was an only child of two traveling circus performers. His mother an "iron-jaw" aerialist, his father a band director. It was called the *Mighty Haag Circus,* and his middle name was chosen in honor of the show. He began his music career as a snare drummer for the Christy Brothers Circus and graduated to a trumpet at the age of eight. At 14 he left the circus and began earning a living as a sideman in a Beaumont, Texas, orchestra. About that time he auditioned for Lawrence Welk. After the try-out, Welk said, "You play too loud for my band." He worked for many small bands until he was picked up by Ben Pollack, the noted jazz drummer. In 1936, Ben Pollack's band was one of the most popular around. Ben discovered Glenn Miller, Charlie Spivak, Benny Goodman, and Jack Teagarden. When Harry was only 20 years old, George Simon mentioned Harry's very good playing in his monthly *Metronome Magazine* column. Benny Goodman's brother, Irving, hired Harry on the spot after listening to him play (on the radio, not in person) just one time. Harry became a star with Goodman. His hot lead trumpet blasted out an almost violent message. When I asked Goodman about Harry, he said, "He ranks with the best brass men in the country. He always had fine ideas when he was with me and they kept improving."

In the recording *Sing, Sing, Sing,* critics said Harry attacked the ears of listeners. They said his improvisation with the trumpet was strange and barbaric. Louis Armstrong once wrote in a letter to author Leonard Feather: "Harry James is another youngster whom won Ol Satch right alongside of a million other fans...His concertos, etc., makes him in my estimation a grand trumpet man...And he can swing too..."(Louis also liked Bunny Berrigan.)

Harry regarded his own style accordingly: "I like and play a rolling style in two-or-four-bar phrasing. To play this way, you know, lots-of-notes-style, you must have a basic knowledge of chords and progressions and perfect control of your instrument." And of technique, he said: "When you make a good, clean start and a 'planted exit, your playing has now acquired spit and polish, so it is only natural that a good beginning will allow you to create more ideas in a free way."

We reminisced about his successful recording of *You Made Me Love You* which first placed him at the top of the charts. "We were in Pittsburgh and having a tough time, so we got on a bus for New York after the last show to open at the Brooklyn Paramount, and when we got there about eight in the morning, there was a big crowd all around the theater, and we wondered what was happening—did somebody kill someone, was there a fire or something? Somebody said, 'Are you kidding? We are waiting to see Harry James." So I said, "How come?" and he says, "Martin Block's been playing *You Made Me Love You* for the last two weeks on the *Make Believe Ballroom* show, and it made the song and the band a hit."

"And you didn't know what was going on till you got there?"

"Didn't have a clue. Block and his show (which was on radio station WNEW in Manhattan from 10 to 12 A.M. every morning) did a lot for us. He liked us...and he never asked for anything in return." The song went on to sell 2.5 million copies and established the band and the song, ending two lean years for the fledging bandleader and his players.

We, of course, talked about that sometimes hard-to-nail-down *favorite recording* question in the interview process: "That's a very difficult thing to say. Only in the last few years have I made recordings I really like. We now record on direct disk for Sheffield Labs (now on C.D.s) and the sound in absolutely fabulous. Before that you heard about 55 percent of what we put in to it and it was always very risky. But my favorite recording was *Trumpet Rhapsody*. It was the most satisfying because it was the most difficult thing I ever played and it did turn out pretty good."

My conversation with Harry James was at a time when Las Vegas casino policy had recently changed to eliminate big bands from the lounges, where Harry had, up to that time, spent a great deal of his playing time. He even moved to Las Vegas to live. That policy forced more traveling for the otherwise young band and at greater distances than Harry was accustomed to.

"Woody Herman told me that all bands are victims of booking agents who throw darts at wall maps."

"True enough, although we never will travel more than 250 miles from job to job. We also get booked in advance and get choices now, not like the old days. That's the band business—if you want the people to see you, you must do it."

"You've been doing this since 1939. That's over 40 years."

"That's also true. But, I'm happy with what I am doing today and I'm happy with what I did yesterday. I live day by day just as long as I'm happy."

"Do you like to play the old stuff?"...I asked, "like *I'm Beginning to See the Light, Two O'clock Jump, All or Nothing at All, I've Heard That Song Before, Flight of the Bumble Bee, Sleepy Lagoon, Ciribiribin*...by the way, Harry, I have to tell you that my lifelong absolute favorite is *I Had the Craziest Dream*" (from the movie *Springtime in the Rockies*).

You have to follow the solo before Helen Forrest takes the vocal. It's that excellent phrasing he does so extraordinarily well that marks Harry James as a great jazz soloist. He was sowing his commercial oats at that time, and I think that Harry also influenced Frank Sinatra's phrasing rather than Tommy Dorsey's trombone as Frank so frequently states. I wondered if Frank realizes that. Harry went on to pursue a progressive jazz policy in later, more financially secure, years.

"Are you a writer or a fan?" He chided me with a grin as I produced original sheet music of my favorite song with a photo of his wife, Betty Grable, Carmen Miranda, John Payne, and Caesar Romero on the cover and handed him a pen for the inevitable signature, something he has repeated for fans thousands of times. He graciously executed the ritual directly over his portion of the photo.

"Haven't seen a copy of this one in years." Then resuming, "We really play what we like, and we play what the people expect us to play. We won't play a tune we don't like—never have made an arrangement of a song I didn't like. Like you and your own favorite (waving the autographed songsheet), the public loves it all."

Historically, the James' band lasted longer under its original leader than any of the others, it being one of the three most popular during the Big Band Era, the others being Glenn Miller and the Benny Goodman orchestras.

Harry James loved to play baseball. He was once considered a promising shortstop by the Detroit Tigers. On the road, the band would play games with rival bands whenever possible. Some say Harry selected musicians first for their ball-playing ability. Some said you had to have a .300 batting average to get an audition with Harry James. Once an avid Brooklyn Dodger fan, he switched to become a great St. Louis Cardinals fan because players like Stan Musial, Enos (Country) Slaughter, and Ray Saunders were supporters of the band and always came out to hear them play.

"Once we pulled off the road for a game and got stuck in a ditch, and it cost me $300 to get towed out and we missed a date that night." Harry once broke his foot sliding into third base during a game and had to conduct the orchestra sitting in a chair with his leg straight out in a cast.

He skirted around and politely avoided conversations of the days when he made those popular movies with ex-wife Betty Grable, who succumbed to cancer in 1973. He would rather talk about his race horses that he ran all over the state of California for so many years. These were more important to him than the Hollywood glory days.

"Harry, I love the story about those two Selmer trumpets you had just bought from the (Selmer) factory in Elkart only the week before when you were on your way to Hollywood to make the movie *Hollywood Hotel*."

Yeah, I remember. I got off the bus with my case under my arm to board the Los Angeles Limited, but I forgot my jacket. I put down the case (a double case for two trumpets), and I went back on the bus, and the bus decided to back up and the wheels turned and ran over both cases with the trumpets inside. It flattened them like a pancake."

"What did you do?"

"I cried!" And we laughed. Benny Goodman bought him two new Selmers when they got to L.A.

In 1979 and 1980 he enjoyed some brisk sales with a couple of new albums, *The King James Version* and *Still Harry After All These Years*. He played very well until the day he died, a great achievement for a horn player. The end came on July 5, 1983, after a short illness at the age of 67. It is said that his friend and former employee, Frank Sinatra, went up to Valley Hospital in Las Vegas to see him shortly before he died, and James told him, "Now I'm going to play trumpet with Gabriel."

When I heard he was in the hospital, I tried calling, to no avail, so I wrote him this letter: *Hello, Harry. Sorry to hear you are under the weather. Hope you are getting better. Thanks for that great interview in 1980 when you told me all your secrets. I have enclosed the article I wrote about you for Long Island P.M. Magazine and a few others pieces written about your great band. You have millions of friends everywhere, like myself, pulling for your recovery. You are more revered and loved than you could ever believe. You have given us a legacy of wonderful music we can listen to all the rest of our lives. By the way, I ran into Ray Anthony a few weeks ago, and I asked him about you and he said you and Louis Armstrong were THE BEST DAMN TRUMPET PLAYERS that ever lived. Boy, that puts you in pretty good company...*

I'm not sure if he ever had the chance to read it.

Harry James in San Francisco in the 1960's.
Photo credit: Mack Harbin collection.

Louis Armstrong All-Stars
Left to Right: Jack Teagarden (trombone), Earl Hines (piano), Barney Bigard (clarinet), Cozy Cole (drums), Louis Armstrong (trumpet), Arvell Shaw (bass), Velma Middleton (vocalist), 1950.

16

Arvell Shaw

And the Louis Armstrong All-Stars Legacy

When his hero, Louis Armstrong, came through St. Louis, Missouri, to play at the Plantation Club back in 1946, Lady Luck was there in full regalia for 22-year-old resident Arvell Shaw. Luckily, Louis's bass player suddenly had to rush home to Philadelphia where his wife was giving birth, creating a need for a replacement bass player to fill the engagement. Armstrong telephoned the union, asking for the best local bass player. Guess who got the job?

Arvell Shaw was born in St. Louis in 1923 and had what he calls an average childhood. His dad was a Protestant minister who had an affection for Louis Armstrong records, especially those Hot Five and Hot Seven's recordings, so Arvell was well exposed to Armstrong's magic. Arvell was playing tuba in a local band for Fate Narable, a former bandmate of Armstrong who had played with him on the riverboats going to and from Alton, Illinois and St. Louis. Fate told many stories of the old days.

"It was my ambition to play someday with such a great musician as Louis Armstrong."

When the Second World War came, armed services representatives visited the all black high schools to recruit black musicians. With the armed forces now integrated, they needed them to fill the newly-created bands for troop entertainment. Arvell joined the Navy and stayed for 3½ years serving in the Pacific. He learned to play the bass fiddle in the Navy band.

It's interesting to note that Louis Armstrong received a similar career break when he was just 17. His own hero, New Orleans trombonist and bandleader, Edward Kid Ory, who had heard about Armstrong's reputation as a cornetist, called on him to replace cornetist King (Joseph) Oliver who had left Kid Ory's Brown Skinned Babies band to go to Chicago on his own. Later, in 1922, Armstrong would join the famous Oliver band, which acted as a catalyst for the development of jazz players. Armstrong's reputation had by that time spread throughout the jazz world, although it's well to point out that earlier Oliver was both teacher and mentor to Armstrong.

Much later on, in 1984, photographer Camille Smith and I were shoehorned in at Sonny's Place on Merrick Road in Seaford, Long Island to interview Arvell Shaw who lives just a few miles away from this busy jazz showcase, a tiny store-front nightclub where owner, Sonny Meyerowitz, still loses his shirt every night in a business that is for him strictly a labor of love. If you glance up at the framed photos on the wall above the bar and tables you will see Count Basie, Louis Armstrong, and others who have graced this hallowed hall. Arvell Shaw is a cuddly bear of a man who embraces his giant bass as a mother envelopes a troubled child. He wears a crisp gray beard and plays with a gentle rocking motion believing every note and every word, loving his work as Armstrong surely loved his.

After playing awhile with Armstrong's big band and just after making the movie, *A Song is Born,* with Danny Kaye, Benny Goodman, Tommy Dorsey and Lionel Hampton, Arvell returned home, but Joe Glaser, Louis' longtime manager, who had disbanded the big band, (many big name bands were closing down at the time) promptly called and asked Arvell if he would be interested in joining Louis Armstrong's newly formed small group at a gig in Billy Berg's nightclub in Los Angeles.

"Is the Pope Catholic?" he replied to Glaser in the affirmative.

"When I got to Berg's I went up close to the marquee and read: 'Louis Armstrong's All Stars, with Jack Teagarden, Barney Bigard,' then below that, Big Sid Catlett, Dick Cary,' and way down at the bottom, 'Arvell Shaw,' and I began to shake. It was an exciting moment for me."

"So, I presume that was the beginning of the Louis Armstrong All-Stars?"

"Yes, it was. And it lasted twenty-five odd years until Louis died in 1971 shortly after completing a two-week engagement at the Waldorf-Astoria in New York. The All-Stars, originally an idea of New York promoter, Ernie Anderson, brought the greatest commercial suc-

Arvell Shaw at Sonny's Place in concert.

cess to Louis Armstrong and his group making him the best-known jazz musician in the world at the time. Arvell left the group for a while in early 1958. Over the years many of the personnel changed for one reason or another. Armstrong also has confessed that he preferred Joe Glaser to choose the musicians that were to play in the group so no one would be offended by Armstrong's personal choices. That way he kept his friends as friends.

After Louis, he toured colleges, played in Broadway's *Bubblin' Brown Sugar,* and joined the band in the show *Ain't Misbehavin'.*

Arvell had just come off tours that included gigs in Germany and England, where, he says, jazz is more widely accepted as the art form. "It's no big deal for seven to eight thousand people to attend a show. Jazz draws the big crowds overseas. It's a shame." he lamented, "...jazz is the most played music in the world today...but not in the U.S. One of the most important art forms of the 20th Century is jazz and it's generally ignored by its own people. It's inexcusable," he went on passionately, "that great musicians have to travel thousands of miles and live away from home to make a living—and rock artists play only about three chords and they're making millions. It's a sick scene that I hope will change."

Of course, all that has changed dramatically since 1984. Jazz patronage is up in the nineties. Now the Grammy wins and other signs of interest are more prevalent. New York and L.A. clubs and music halls regularly feature jazz ensembles and tributes to departed fellow-musicians, with leading artists, including Arvell Shaw who named his group 'The Louis Armstrong Legacy Band' in tribute to his old boss.

During that Germany tour which included pianist Teddy Wilson, vibraphonist Red Norvo, guitarist Tal Farlow, tenor sax artist Buddy Tate, trumpeter Billy Butterfield, and clarinetist Johnny Mince, Teddy Wilson became ill: "I'll tell you what happened. We were in a restaurant when Teddy got up to go to the bathroom and he suddenly just collapsed. He turned gray and couldn't breath. We figured he had a heart attack so we called an ambulance. They thought he had bleeding ulcers because he was losing blood for so long. Then, after tests were taken, they said he had cancer. He stayed in the hospital for three weeks and they flew him to Boston. (Teddy passed on in 1986 from that illness.) Johnny Mince and I went on to England with Johnny Guarnieri (pianist), Barrett Deems (drums), Ed Hubble (trombonist), and Keith Smith, an English trumpet player who sounds so much like Louis you can't tell them apart., The group was named *The Hundred Years of American and Dixieland Jazz Band.*

And, like his old boss, Arvell Shaw began to sing. It started when he was appearing in Oslo, Norway when one of the musicians bet he wouldn't sing during his featured spot. "So I went out and announced to the ten thousand people at this concert that I would like to sing. I looked back at Louis and he rolled up his eyes and he looked like he was thinking, 'this cat is crazy', and I sang *St. James Infirmary,* the only song I knew all the lyrics to and the house came down. I began singing seriously about two years ago and the people liked it so I said, maybe I have something here." Now he sings at every performance. His solo rendition of *Yesterdays* is worth the trip alone. But, he's a better bassist.

Although Armstrong was a very innovative and excellent musician, (as Teddy Wilson once said, "He had balance and tone. Harmonic sense. Excitement. Technical skill. Originality.)" he considered himself mainly an entertainer. Jazz aficionados saw him as an important jazz musician, but he preferred all around entertaining, not just exclusively performing jazz material. Projecting his personality was important to him as was singing and recording with people like Bing Crosby and Ella Fitzgerald.

The change for Armstrong, from virtuoso jazz performer to singer and entertainer, happened after an eighteen month European tour that ended with a split lip in 1935. Some say it was musical deterioration, others swear he could play just as good, but he simply choose the vaudeville style of performing much to the dismay of jazz purists. Following in Armstrong's footsteps, Arvell Shaw had arrived at a similar crossroads: To be just a musician, or a homogeneous entertainer?

Over those many years, Armstrong would always take care of his protegé: "He had no children of his own, and he wouldn't show me any affection openly. But, if things would go wrong for me, he would say 'Leave him alone!' or 'Give him this or that,' and 'Let him do this or that'."

21

Louis and friend, circa 1950.

When former bandleader, a star in his own right, Earl "Fatha" Hines replaced All-Star Dick Cary at the piano, young Arvell found another friend and mentor: "Earl was great because he really believed in helping young musicians and would spend time and give them a chance. He took me under his wings, helped me, and taught me about all aspects of show business. You know, he did a lot for Sarah Vaughan and Billy Eckstine back in the old days."

Arvell said that Armstrong loved making movies. "Did you catch the scene in *High Society* where Bing Crosby introduces all us All-Stars (Trummy Young—trombone, Ed Hall—clarinet, Billy Kyle—piano, Barrett Deems—drums, Arvell, and Louis) in the song scene *Now You Has Jazz*? Of course I had, the whole world has. Arvell and the other members of the group took their licks on a specialty solo while Bing and Louis vocalized and Louis wrapped up the number in a stunning finish with Bing wailing and flinging his arms around like never before. It was the best Crosby/Armstrong jazz duet ever.

So Arvell and his close association with perhaps the greatest jazz musician of the century has helped him carve out a niche of his own in the world of music he loves so well. But instead of struggling as just a studio or pickup musician, he has established an elité group of his own, although the marketplace is different now and the tours scant in comparison to those past glory days.

"To survive, you must change and grow constantly, Arvell pointed-ed out. "It's always been true, but I don't discard anything if it's good. I still listen and learn most everytime out. You cannot become stagnant or you will die. Woody Herman taught me that. I'm sixty (actually seventy-one in 1995) now and I will always keep on learning and working. I'll keep going till I die. I'll never find myself pacing the floor looking for something or other to do. My music keeps me young and keeps me happy. The older you get, the more effort it takes. (chuckling) But it still keeps you alive and the musical adrenaline cooking."

It's November of 1995 now and he's still very much at it, we are happy to report. Arvell's performing a jazz concert with his All-Stars at the Adams Playhouse at Hofstra University in Hempstead, Long Island, for the benefit of P.L.U.S. Group homes for Autistic Adults. This is his twelfth year at the project which was started by his late

Giving pointers to Louis Armstrong's All-Star, Arvell Shaw, at Sonny's Place in Long Island.

wife, Madeleine, for the original benefit of his only child and other deserving people.

Jazz is still full of challenges for Arvell Shaw. He has contributed buoyant tone and impeccable continuity to a host of stellar players throughout his long career and keeps on going, the ultimate tribute to his beloved friend and fellow entertainer, Louis Armstrong, who will always be considered the most important trumpeter in the history of jazz.

The Andrews Sisters' Patty Andrews.

It's Apple Blossom Time

Patty, Maxene, & LaVerne

I have always been in love with the Andrews Sisters. Ever since I first heard Patty, Maxene, & LaVerne vocalize *Bie Mir Bist Du Schoen,* it was the beginning of my long-running affection for them. The three gals from Minneapolis belonged to me from that day forward. They were my personal entertainers. Their recordings punctuated my life at many meaningful milestones. For me, and for millions of others, during World War II and later into the fifties, they were the definitive female strains of the era.

When Patty would take that solo with her special delivery, timbre and clarity very few singers possessed, I just dissolved. When they recorded my favorite, *Rumors Are Flying*, and Patty did that doubling-up-jive patter with such melodic perfection, *Whatta-ya-do-do-do—that keeps em buzzing*...I couldn't wait until the record was over so I could lift the arm and play it again and again, and wait for those passages to enter my brain once more. They really had me hooked.

When I initiated my search for Patty Andrews in 1984, I had almost given up until I finally obtained the telephone number of her manager, Wally Weschler. So, that evening from my office, I placed the call and a woman with a familiar ring to her voice answered with a sweet, "Hello, who is it?"

"Hi," said I, and I identified myself, "is this the office of Wally Weschler?"

"Why, Yes!"

"Well, I'm actually looking for Patty Andrews," I inquired.

"It's me...it's Patty!" was the bubbling reply.

"*Patty Andrews*?" I repeated in disbelief and relief.

"Yeah!" she shouted.

Well, it was too easy. I had found another of my heroes. Wally turned out to be her husband, manager, & musical director.

By her own description, Patty is a very happy and busy girl living in a beautiful, Tudor-style house near Encino, California. She regularly works the California concert circuit with band leaders, Tex Beneke (once Glenn Miller's favorite sax player, and vocalist on the first gold record, *Chattanooga Choo-Choo)*, musical genius, Larry Elgart, and the Harry James Orchestra at places like the Hollywood Palladium. Her concerts consist of new and refreshing popular songs, but she always finishes off a concert with some of the Andrew Sisters' routines of the earlier songs.

After some small talk, Patty and I settled down to talk about the Andrews Sisters. When they were only teenagers attending dancing school, they began mimicking the then-popular Boswell Sisters, who flourished from the late twenties until they broke up in 1936, with Connie continuing on as a soloist. They, like Patty, the youngest, Maxene, a few years older, and LaVerne, the oldest, were actual sisters too.

The girls entered the *Kiddy Reviews* during the summer months on the Orpheum Theater Circuit in Minneapolis. Larry Rich, one of the headliners in the vaudeville show invited the girls to become a permanent part of his show touring the country on the R.K.O.(Radio-Keith-Orpheum) circuit. They would perform 4 to 5 shows a day sandwiched between movie showings. Not having their own charts or any special arranger, they copied the Boswell arrangements.

"When you are young, there is always someone you look up to," she said, "so we did what they did and it helped launch our career. We would sing things like *Shuffle Off to Buffalo,* and *When I Take My Sugar to Tea,* and *I Found A Million Dollar Baby in A Five And Ten Cents Store."*

The girls had no formal training, but their enthusiasm and devotion to the Boswell's kept them going and eventually brought them to their own accomplished, personal style. Patty sang the lead and solo parts, Maxene the high harmony, and LaVerne took the third part.

"We would work all day until we perfected new songs in our own new, bouncier style. It was then we realized we had something special to offer."

28

The girls never took singing lessons: "It wasn't until many years later—after problems with laryngitis—that I finally had to take (singing) lessons to learn how to breathe properly in order to prevent damage to my vocal chords," Patty explained.

"Then one day upon reaching St. Paul, Leon Belasco, a big band leader, heard of us—came to see the show and offered us more money. We were making thirty dollars a week and he would raise it to fifty if we would join up with him." Patty related, "So just like (Frank) Sinatra left Harry James to join Tommy Dorsey to make enough money to live on—we joined Belasco. But," she added, "the band broke up when we got to New York and the only job we could get was singing on the radio twice a week with Billy Swanson's Band at the Hotel Edison."

This was to be the girls' first big break. Dave Kapp, Vice President of Decca Records, heard them while traveling crosstown in a cab and went directly to the hotel where Patty was sitting in the lobby during a break. He handed her his card and asked her to show up the next day at Decca.

"It was the beginning of an association that lasted 17 years. "she noted triumphantly.

Jack Kapp, however, was the creative genius behind the Decca label.

"He was young and aggressive and like a father to us young girls. He was Dave's older brother and President of the company. It was Jack who got us to record with Bing Crosby and later to make movies with the Ritz Brothers, Abbott and Costello, and with Bob Hope and Bing.

Their first big recording was taken from an old Yiddish song with English words added by Sammy Cahn and Saul Chaplin. *Bie Mir Bist Du Shoen* became a commercial success.

"It's funny, "She added, "We only got fifty dollars—me and my sisters—and our mom *and* dad—for recording that song." laughing as she reminisced. Then I recounted the story of how Fran Warren told me she received only fifty dollars for recording her classic, *Sunday Kind of Love* with Claude Thornhill.

"But she didn't have to split it five ways!" Patty always sparkles when she relates these little tidbits. "But we later wrote a better contract with Decca." However, just like Fran, this was to be the catalyst in their career.

Soon they released a constant barrage of wonderful recordings that were rhythmic, bouncy, and gutsy—not to exclude that 40's expression—"jivey." They swept the country: *Joseph, Joseph,* and *Oh, Ma Ma (He Wants to Marry Me),* in 1938 were both successful. So were *Hold Tight, Billy Boy, Beer Barrel Polka, Well, All Right,* and their first recordings with Bing, *Ciribiribin, Oh! Johnny, Oh!* and *South America Take It Away,* in 1939.

In those takes, Bing took the solo and the girls took the choruses: "We loved recording with Bing. It was always so exciting. He always used to do a little something unexpected, like the time he sneaked in that line at the end of *Pistol Packin' Momma*—'Lay that thing down before it goes off and hurts someone.' He broke us up. We were a complement to each other," she mused. "Bing would always record at eight in the morning," she revealed. "I guess he used to vocalize in the car on the way to the studio—and he always wore his golf clothes. He claimed his voice had a husky quality in the morning."

Bing never did more than one take on any of the more than fifty sides the girls recorded with him. "Bing believed you had the best enthusiasm the first time, although I secretly believe he did it so he could get out on the golf course earlier."

In 1940 the hits were, *Hit the Road, Beat Me Daddy Eight to the Bar,* the definitive *I'll Be With You in Apple Blossom Time,* and another one of those favorites of mine, *Ferry Boat Serenade...*(you know..."I love to ride the ferry, Where people are so merry. There's a man that plays the concert-ina, On the moonlight upper dec-or-ina.") And how about the famous *Boogie Woogie, Bugle Boy (from Company 'B')* from the Abbott and Costello film *Buck Privates* which all added most agreeably to their musical skyrocket. (Bette Midler was to make a recording of that song in the early nineties all with an idea of making a film of the girls with Bette as Patty, but it never materialized.) All their songs and arrangements during this period were selected by Dave Kapp, who was also the girls A & R (artists and repertoire) man.

30

"He was even able to choose our movie songs. That's how songs like *Aurora, Yes, My Darling Daughter, and Daddy (I Want A Diamond Ring)* became ours to sing."

Kapp was able to have the girls record with Al Jolson, Dick Haymes, Bob Crosby, Woody Herman, Carmen Miranda, Jimmy Dorsey, and even Danny Kaye. The song *Any Bonds Today* which they recorded in 1941, helped immeasurably with the sale of Defense Bonds. The girls also sang regularly at Armed Forces Camps, U.S.O.'s, and The Stage Door Canteens which were sort of night clubs where armed forces personnel could go cost-free and meet movie stars and other famous celebrities when on liberty or leave.

In 1942 came the memorable *Don't Sit Under the Apple Tree*, the bouncy *Pennsylvania Polka,* and one of the most stirring World War II songs ever recorded, *When Johnny Comes Marching Home.* The very mention of that tune recalled wartime life for me as an 11 year old in Brooklyn, New York: the waiting lines for sugar and meat—handing in those ration stamps and tokens that were part of the food rationing program, and the frightening wail of the blackout sirens even though it was always practice. Patty remembered it too. "Especially when you couldn't get nylons—we had to beg our friends. You didn't wear slacks then, so you needed those stockings."

Then came their best-selling, best known song, *Rum & Coca Cola.* It sold over 7 million copies, which was a great feat in the wartime forties with the shortage of shellac, the raw-material that made the 78's. It was a song recorded only because there was 15 minutes of radio time left to use up and it was "...just stuck in," Patty recalled. "It was recorded by chance."

The demand for that recording was so great that both RCA and Columbia Records gave up their shellac allotment in order to allow Decca to meet the demand.

On a later album with Gordon Jenkins and his orchestra, Patty was soloist on *I Want To Be Loved,* and she absolutely excelled on *It Never Entered My Mind.* Here is Patty Andrews at her phonetic and melodic best. It is so pure, and performed so perfectly. Patty was indeed the leader of the girls and all the sounds must be channeled through the leader. The Andrews Sisters succeeded because of Patty's leadership and soloing.

31

The girls performed at the London Palladium in 1950, and eventually broke up a few years later. But, in-between they performed on their own radio program and made many motion pictures: *Stage Door Canteen, The Road to Utopia* (with you know Who), *In the Navy, Buck Privates, Argentine Nights,* and *Follow the Boys.*

"We had such fun with Bob and Bing when we did the 'Road' pictures," Patty added, "Bob and Bing would each have their own gag writers on the set and would sneak in special gags and lines and throw them at each other in front of the cameras. And they were kept in too—you can tell—if you look closely—they always surprised each other."

Patty responded to that inescapable inquiry about naming her favorite recording:

"It's like a mother with 5 children. You can't say what's your favorite."

At this writing, Patty, because of unknown personal reasons, was not exactly friendly with her sister, Maxene, who lived in Manhattan, and had written a book recently about all their lives and fortunes, but without Patty's cooperation. Maxene had also become active in clubs in the last year or two. Her last performance was earlier this year in Honolulu at the 50th Anniversary of the end of World War II. She died just two days ago, as I was writing this chapter, on October 22, 1995. LaVerne passed on in 1967.

Patty is truly grateful for an abundant and fruitful career and clearly acknowledges her debt to her fans, young and old alike. I always sent Patty newspapers clippings about her sister in hopes that it would spark an interest, but for that unknown reason, they never reconciled their differences. Patty and I still exchange Christmas cards and little notes from time to time. We're fortunate to have the recordings of the Andrew Sisters, which will probably be used by female group singers as a measure of their own abilities for many years to come.

Shortly after my first Andrews Sisters interview was published in *Long Island PM Magazine,* Patty called me at my office to offer thanks and to tell me from that day on, the article would be used to sell her act. That was July 18, 1985. She is still singing her heart out.

Band Leader Ray Anthony makes a point.

Ray Anthony

Not Always in the Footsteps of Tradition

Raymond Antonini of Bentleyville, Pa. came by his music naturally:

"My dad taught me when I was five years old. He started me on the trumpet, so I'm from a musical family."

Ray Anthony, as he is known to all of us, starred first in the Antonini Family Orchestra, comprised of his sister, two brothers and dad. "Then I started and played in my own band when I was just fourteen. The other players were in their twenties and thirties. I was way ahead of my time."

During high school, Ray played trumpet with local bands and quickly rose to the point where he was working as a featured trumpeter with Al Donohue's fine orchestra in Boston. At the age of 18 he joined Jimmy Dorsey and then became a member of the distinguished Glenn Miller Orchestra.

"I guess you had to play pretty good to land a job with Glenn Miller," I said to him during our conversation held at radio station WLIM on Long Island where he was a guest of veteran Big Band radio jock and co-owner of the station, Jack Ellsworth.

"I was a lot better than I even knew myself because...yes, you're right, Glenn Miller is not going to hire you because of your looks, or anything else except what you can do on your instrument. He was the number one band and asked me to audition for him while I was with Donohue's band. I guess he heard of me, so I thought I must be pretty good."

"Then why did you leave the band so quickly afterwards?"

"He fired me."

"He *what*?" I was really surprised.

35

With a thoughtful grin and a shake of the right shoulder: "He fired me."

"Why?"

"Well, that's hard to say. I don't think I was a bad guy, but I was obviously cocky...it might have been plain enthusiasm, you know, me being so young—and so excited to be there that I did things that didn't fall into line and I did other things like auditioning for Benny Goodman and Artie Shaw just for the kick of doing it."

"Guess Glenn might have resented that," I said.

"Well that might have been a kick for me, but he obviously didn't like it—and that actually only crossed my mind in the last so many years...that it was one of the dumb things I did as a kid. But, he re-hired me a few months later because my influence in the brass section was a strong one." I later learned that he was let go by Miller, after a New York engagement at the Cafe Rouge, (mostly to save money) and he was rehired again in Cleveland when the band came through and Miller realized he was a better player than his replacement, Ralph Brewster.

"It's known that he admired your energy and enthusiasm and that you remained as a member of the band for a few years."

"Yes, but he fired me again," laughing out loud now, "Glenn was a disciplinarian whether it was in your playing, your mannerisms, or what you wore on the bandstand, he wanted and expected the best. He offered the people his best and I had a great respect for him. He was also, like Lawrence Welk, tight with a buck although he paid me enough, and his featured players like Beneke too, but other players weren't so happy." I then remembered Woody Herman telling me about Glenn's great financial losses on the long, rocky road to eventual success. Perhaps that was the reason he was so frugal, he had lots of practice.

"I guess you were satisfied playing in that band with his kind of music because you emulated him in your future band when you got out of the Navy after the war."

"Oh, yes! Well his music was the most accepted by the American GI's so when I started up my new band back in Cleveland, I re-styled it for that reason," he explained. I believe that when Ralph Flanagan started the parade of Glenn Miller mimics, Ray fell in line and, like

Talking Big Band with Ray Anthony at WLIM Radio.

the other imitators, made good money touring at many of the country's top spots, then went on to record for Capitol and built and promoted a good swinging band, featuring his own gutsy, low-registering horn.

Ray was also influenced earlier by his idols Harry James and Louis Armstrong: "They were the best damned trumpet players ever. Harry played sweet, pretty, fast, hot, high or low—everything that is possible to do on the horn. He was the one of the best players of all time." He said all that with strong emotion. "And Louis...what can you say...he influenced every trumpet player including me and Harry James."

"I know Harry James is a friend, but did you ever *tell* him that?"

Pause and reflection: "I don't know if I have—or not. But we talk about other things. You don't talk about *that*. And, as far as a jazz influence is concerned, Roy Eldridge stands alone as my teacher."

In those postwar years Ray was one of the fastest-rising new dance bands, despite the fact that the overall band business was in decline. When he was performing on the Nevada circuit for twenty years, (1960's to 1980's) he had a small group show called the *Bookend Revue* with two female vocalist/dancers that played the lounges of Las Vegas and Lake Tahoe, then traveled to Acapulco, and Honolulu where he appeared at the Royal Hawaiian Hotel.

Ray also pioneered his craft by offering original music themes for some television shows in the 60's. His best-selling recordings of *Dragnet* and *Peter Gunn* are nothing short of sensational. During the years 1950 through 1954, Ray Anthony was voted Number One Band in all the trade magazine polls and during the same period, was the most played instrumental recording artist on radio. The seventies saw Ray with his show *Directions 71* which combined the best sounds of the big bands with current stylings. He was always an innovator with vision.

In the mid-eighties Ray returned to touring from the state of Texas to Hackensack, New Jersey: "The jobs are where they are and you have to go to them, that's always been true. That's where the people will be able to see you and get to know you. It's great to play to different crowds."

Ray also started up a nationwide mail-order business selling newly re-issued original recordings through something called Big Bands Eighties where he would ship recordings everywhere. "We perpetuated it all by compiling a list of radio stations and big band fans and produced an LP featuring myself and five other big bands (Harry James, Woody Herman, Sammy Kaye, Freddy Martin, and Les Elgart) playing two tracks each and shipped it to 500 stations. People would call in and inquire where they could buy the records they just heard on the radio and, since there were few places to send them, they recommended Big Bands Eighty. With 2,500 listings, we're just like a store that buys and re-sells."

Well, this band leader, movie star, television performer, occasional stage actor, and entrepreneur is still a pretty busy guy these days. He is concentrating on those record sales, leading his band on weekends here and there, and still making albums, the last two featuring the Glenn Miller sound on song titles never recorded before.

Though active, Ray Anthony is leading a relatively quiet life lately. He's a nine-to-fiver doing mail order and his whole social life is centered around tennis and hanging out with friend, Hugh Hefner at the Playboy Mansion. "We always have dinner and sometimes watch old movies. Mel Torme and (comedian) Chuck McCann hang out with us—as we get a little older, all of us, we kind of find comfort in the friendship of people we've known for many years."

Syndicated radio's *Big Band Jump* director and commentator Don Kennedy, whose famous *Newsletter* I've written for frequently, recently asked Ray how he felt about getting older: "Getting old starts in your mind. You have to get old in your mind before your body'll get old. At least in my case, and in a lot of cases, if your mind gets old, your body's gonna follow. I don't think much about it, but I'm so busy that it's not of importance to me. I do need glasses to read...and I sometimes get forgetful...In fact, who *are* you, anyway?"

Methinks Ray Anthony will keep going 'til he drops.

With my friend and mentor Frankie Laine.

Mr. Rhythm

Frank Paul Lo Vecchio Takes to the Mike

It's difficult for me to believe that my friend Frankie Laine almost gave up on his fledgling singing career, actually taking out two and a half years to work at a defense plant where he earned a steady sixty-eight dollars a week. Then with a few bucks in his pocket, he returned to the fray to try again but promising himself to quit if he did not succeed on his next bid.

But, of course, he probably never would have stopped, no matter what he may have said at the time. I think I know Frank pretty well now, and his determination and dedication to his craft were always unwavering, good times and bad, to say the least. The admirable way Frank has conducted his personal and professional life in every respect since his very first success in 1946 at that infamous Hollywood hangout on Vine Street, *Billy Berg's*, I'm sure, with dedication and his exemplary motivation, he would have hung on until his career turned itself around:

"I was invited to sit in one night and I came away with good luck for a change by singing *Old Rocking Chair's Got Me*. My luck turned, because a guy in the audience got very excited about the way I sang it, and he turned out to be the song's composer, Hoagy Carmichael (also the composer of *Stardust*), who got Billy to give me a job." (Frank started at $75.00 a week.)

Frank was the first he-man singer...other than country-western singers—who the blue-collar guys could identify with, but he really had a hard time and some bad luck along the way.

"Earlier," he went on, "my friend, (well-known bandleader) Jean Goldkette, got me a job at NBC, but England decided to declare war on Germany that day and my job went out the window. Hell, I was already 26 years old then. I hung around Ted Weems' band while my

41

pal, Perry Como was his singer. Perry recommended me for his replacement when he was leaving, but Weems didn't accept it (Frank sang *Never in A Million Years* at his audition, which turned out to be prophetic) so Perry got me a job with his old boss, bandleader Freddie Carlone. That lasted just a few weeks because my jazz style didn't match his sweet Guy Lombardo type of band." Frank's style was very innovative, which was why he had such difficulty with early acceptance. He would bend notes and sing about the chordal context of a note rather than to sing the note directly, and he stressed each rhythmic downbeat, which was different than the smooth balladeer of his time.

When he sang at Cleveland's College Inn in 1940, Frank humanely introduced an unknown, starving singer, June Hart, who he really thought was terrific and needed a break. They actually hired *her* to replace *him*. More bad luck while helping someone, but that's Frank. However, she sang a ballad entitled *That's My Desire*, which Frank liked very much, but unfortunately forgot about for six years.

"And how about the time I was ready to sing a benefit at the Congress Hotel in Chicago when suddenly Roy Eldridge showed up and decided to go into *Body and Soul*. Who'd dare interrupt that for a punk kid nobody even knew?"

Fortunately, he decided to try out his terrific version of *That's My Desire,* with head thrown back, eyes closed and mike in hand later while at Billy Berg's. It brought down the house and began his climb up the ladder to success. Then he began recording those he-man hits one after another, first with Mercury and then on Columbia: *That's My Desire,* then *Lucky Old Sun, Jezebel, Mule Train, Shine, High Noon, Cry of the Wild Goose, Moonlight Gambler,* and *Rawhide*...all memorable—all number-one smash hits, and to prove his bonafide affinity to country music, how about his definitive interpretation of Hank Williams' *Your Cheatin' Heart.*

What enthusiastic recordings! But, as good as they were, I much prefer Frank's inspiring, early rendition of *We'll Be Together Again,* (which he wrote with his lifelong friend, Carl Fischer) and the prayerlike, *I Believe*, the latter his own personal favorite and actually an expression of his definition of life.

Helen O'Connell's affection for discoverer and friend, Frankie Laine.

I first saw Frankie Laine at the New York Paramount in 1947. He was on the in-person show with Ray McKinley and comedian Billy DeWolfe, during the run of the movie *Golden Earrings*. My first meeting with Frank was in 1983 backstage at Long Island's Westbury Music Fair. He was appearing with his discovery, and now old friend, Helen O'Connell, Moe Zudicoff (better known as bandleader Buddy Morrow, who was fronting the Tommy Dorsey ghost band.) and William B. Williams of New York's WNEW and its famous radio show, *Make Believe Ballroom,* an oldtime, long-running, classic disk-jockey program that best represented the Big Band Era. We hit it off like old friends at a reunion, which was easy to do. I felt like I knew him since high school because it was through his recordings that he made you *feel that way*. After a few minutes together, we rounded up Helen O'Connell from the ladies dressing room and quickly cleared up how he first *discovered* Helen:

"Well, Jimmy Dorsey's secretary, Nita Moore, and I were having breakfast and she told me that Jimmy was looking for a girl singer. (Helen was nodding her head up and down.) It happened that I saw Helen the night before singing at the Village Barn down on Eighth Street and I told Nita about her and Jimmy went to see her that night, and that's how he got Helen O'Connell." Helen was standing right next to me and Frank when he related that story with Helen nodding approval, then snuggling up and planting a kiss on Frank's blushing cheek. Photographer, Camille Smith, with a keen nose for a photo-op, quickly snapped it for the record. (When Helen was asked by Camille to face me nose-to-nose for a photo, she looked at me and blurted out, *"Do I Have to?"*)

Frank told me about his phenomenal success when he was appearing in England, where he is so revered by the populace. On opening night at the Palladium, August 18, 1952, he broke the attendance record previously held by Judy Garland and Danny Kaye. He was sold out for the entire length of his stay (two weeks) and even the standing-room only places, which were sold the day of each show, sold out the fastest ever in the theater's history. The crowds milled outside the Palladium before each show. Nan and Frank were thrilled to death. It was so much more than they expected so far from home. It was then that he received a phone call from Mitch Miller, his producer from

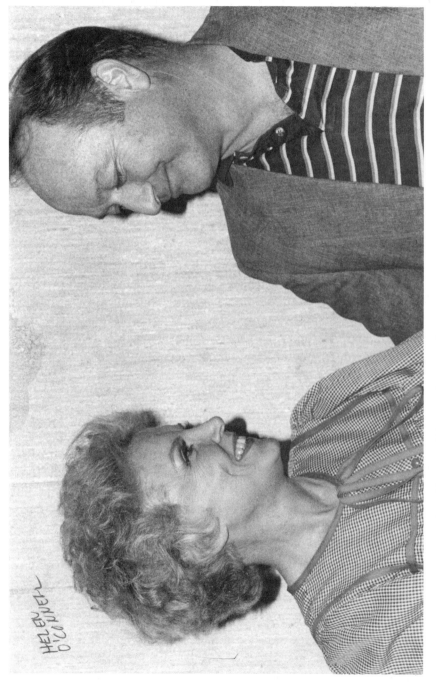

"Do I have to?" says Helen O'Connell when asked to face me.

45

Columbia Records, telling him his recording of *Mule Train* and *High Noon* were released in the states and were a smash. Carl Fischer improvised an arrangement from what he remembered of *Mule Train*, and the next night they stuck the song in the act. The audience went crazy.

Frank's version of *High Noon* is really the definitive record, although it was Tex Ritter who sang the song on the film. A lot of people expect to hear Frank when they view the film.

Frank went on to Glasgow, Scotland, and opened at the Empire Theater to an incredible reception. A crowd of over 5000 people gathered outside their hotel and would not go away until Frank went out on the balcony and sang a few bars of *Rock of Gibraltor,* a song that went over big in Britain. Frank has always appreciated his fans. And they know he understands them, too.

Frank went on to Italy to sing *Jezebel* to a screaming crowd everywhere he travelled in his parents' place of birth. Appearances in Milan, Venice, Florence, and Rome, where crowds topped each previous performance, were equally exciting for the travelling performer from America. He and Nan were genuinely overwhelmed at all the attention given them overseas. In France, where he renewed his friendship with singer, Edith Piaf, known to the world as *The Little Sparrow*, Frankie and Nan were followed by crowds of fans everywhere they visited. *Jezebel* had been a big hit in France.

Frank returned to Europe over and over to even greater successes. He has recorded hundrds of titles over the years, and his international record sales exceeded the 100,000,000 mark long ago.

In his book *"That Lucky Old Son,"* Frank recalls that special feeling, corny though he thought it was, on returning a success to New York, where he once felt the lowest point of his career. "I promised myself that I wouldn't come back to New York unless I could do so 'on a white horse'." He couldn't forget the nights sleeping in Central Park and the days that dragged by for him without food.

"That's why I made it a point to treat myself to one very special evening during my first run at the Paramount. I spent it alone. I donned a custom-made suit and a camel's-hair overcoat and headed for Central Park. There, I sought out the dilapidated bench that had once been my bed. I sat down and ate a candy bar and thought about the time when penny candy bars were all I could afford to eat. In one of my pockets sat a loaded wallet, in the other a key to one of the most comfortable hotel suites in New York. After a while I hailed a taxi and drove to the heart of Times Square, where my name was in big, beautiful lights and they were paying me $2500 a week to do what I loved best." Frank hopes that everybody, at least once in their lives, knows such a moment for themselves.

In 1985, while I was penning a monthly column called "Jazz and Jazzmen" for *Long Island P.M.,* Frank fell ill with a quadruple-bypass heart operation. I let the readers know and invited them to write letters of encouragement to Frank at his San Diego home that overlooked the harbor. He was so grateful.

Frank had a remarkable recovery and by the time 1990 rolled around, he had completed his fifth year since the surgery, but in April of 1990 he had to have a triple bypass. In 1991, however, Frank was having some throat troubles and took a year off. His good wife of then 42 years, the former movie actress Nan Grey, had troubles with her vision which, by way of two operations, was fully restored to 20/20.

Now, a few years later, with Nan gone, Frank continues performing benefits for Meals on Wheels, and other Human Health Services Agency programs that help seniors, as needed, and he is recording a new CD album at this writing with songs like *Scarlet Ribbons* and *When Sunny Gets Blue.* Frank is promoting his newly written autobiography *That Lucky Old Son* with book signings all over California. (I was delighted to receive an autographed copy right after publication.)

"Nan's special way of touching my life will remain in my heart forever and lets me go on to do my work. I *believe,*" he says so sincerely, "*God* is everywhere. You don't have to go to church to find him."

Frank has one of the biggest hearts in show business and one of the smallest egos. Frank's last words in his book are, like the song says…"*the music never ends.*" That's the best legacy Frankie Laine can ever give us.

Count William Basie, circa 1966. Photo credit: Big Band Jump.

The Kid from Redbank

The Band Was Like Some Great Locomotive

On a bitter cold evening in February of 1982, my wife, Jeanette, and I set out to meet Count William James Basie, the enduring piano player from Red Bank, New Jersey, who led the longest-running jazz institution at the even older Northstage Theater in Glen Cove, Long Island, where he was appearing with his band for one of those one-nighters. We had heard Bill Basie was ailing and had even ordered a mechanical wheelchair. But that didn't stop him from performing. When I spoke to him by telephone at his hotel just a few days before, he asked us not to bring any cameras. We couldn't help but wonder...why?

The Northstage stage entrance was dark, the stagedoor decrepit, and the backstage facilities simply bleak, cold, and bare. It was hard to believe the great Count Basie was to use these facilities this night. We waited around, talking to band member and breathtaking player, Freddie Green, the veteran Basie guitarist who has been with him since 1937, the acknowledged true pulse of the band.

When Basie and his party arrived, cold winds blew in behind them further chilling the backstage corridor the old steam radiators could not too adequately heat. We directed them to the largest and warmest dressing room. Catherine, Basie's wife of over 40 years, literally was holding him steady. He held a cane for added support. He look wasted, physically diminished, but cheerful and even enthusiastic, still his life and vitality was indeed waning. Now we understood why the "no cameras." He had a severe case of arthritis of the spine and had a 1976 heart attack, but it was pancreatic cancer that ended his life just a few short years later.

While Jeanette and Catherine got to know one another, Bill, his valet and I sipped some Chablis and talked about the Count's great career. At one point we had to excuse the women, while we helped Bill change from street clothes to stage clothes. He placed his hands across my shoulders as he attempted to stand up and received added assistance from his valet until we finally got him dressed for the performance. Friends and acquaintances showed up, popped in their heads for a handshake or a glass of Chablis that the theater manager cheerfully furnished. The manager also handed him a fistful of cash which Basie waved over his head like the winner in a crap game, then pocketed it with a grin.

We began the taped interview talking about the myriad Basie personnel, a who's who of jazz artists who played or sung with him over the years: Lester Young, Illinois Jacquet, Harry Sweets Edison, Clark Terry, Jo Jones, Roy Eldridge, Benny Carter, Buddy Tate, Stan Getz, Buddy De Franco, Lucky Thompson, and singers Jimmy Rushing, Helen Humes, and Joe Williams. I chided him about his three-noted signature, the beguiling "Plink, Plank, Plink" piano ending and he simply smiled and explained that it was a trademark. "You know," he said, "just like Bing's 'bub-bub-boo,' but our band is like some great locomotive then it ends quiet-like, you know."

And when I asked him why he keeps on turning out for those grueling one night stands, he simply replied, "Got to eat—just like you—got to pay my rent and go to the super market, you know!" And about his accession to the rank of "Count," he confirmed that it was a radio announcer in Kansas City, deciding that he was on a par with "Duke" Ellington, and "King of Swing" Benny Goodman, who dubbed him accordingly.

As almost any longtime Basie fan can tell you, his great fantasy as a young leader was "to go on the road touring everywhere." It was his great fortune to put the talent and fantasy together in a career that lasted longer than most people's entire lives.

Basie spoke endearingly about his one-time, magical vocalist, Billie Holiday, who spent one year or so with the band early-on (he was 34 and she was 25) and concluded with: "She and I kinda almost started up together—you know." lowering his voice to escape Catherine's range, but didn't make it. Catherine delivered an understanding and knowing smile and the wry comment: "Well, I don't know about that!" as Bill looked quickly away. The only recordings Billie made with Basie were those rare radio broadcast air checks performed at the Savoy Hotel, just before she went over to Artie Shaw.

I asked if he ever played any other instrument besides his beloved piano. Basie said that he liked the drums and once auditioned with the original "Dixieland Band," "but they asked for the sticks back"...and when I asked him who his mentor or hero was, Fats Waller was a noted number one: "I used to watch him in the first row play organ for the silent movies and fell in love with him right away."

On more serious subjects, I confronted him about cigarettes, alcohol, and even drugs, to which so many musicians have succumbed, but which he put a stop to almost twenty years ago, and he never engaged the latter: "Was easy. The doctor told me to stop, and I stopped...gradual like, but I stopped. Never touched the other stuff...and it's not fair to say that just musicians use drugs." I think he felt offended or was defending.

"Do you prefer the work you do today, maybe those dynamic Neal Hefti arrangements, or the hard-swinging stuff, or do you think it was the early band that was your favorite?" to the answer: "I liked the first band (it made him immortal), but the new band (since 1952) made me some money." "And what's your favorite piece?" "Why, One O'Clock Jump, of course—you kiddin, don't you know that?" Of course, we did.

But what about April in Paris? "It's nice too," he said.

Over the years Basie perfected his light, swinging style with a beat that is always there, and, unlike most bands, he placed an emphasis on simple, hummable riffs which appeal to everyone because the music can be easily understood: "Is your playing really pretty much the same as it was a long time ago?" "Sure," he explained, "There is no other way," his voice rising emphatically. We left Bill and Catherine to the crowd, now building up inside the theater. After this session and one later at the Jones Beach summer theater, the Basie's were headed for their Bahamas retreat.

If there was a Pulitzer for music, Basie deserves it more than anyone. He employed more worthy musicians, he changed the direction of the sounds of jazz by allowing his players to use the devices they employed best with their instruments in a undisciplined manner, unlike Ellington who worked his stricter arrangements around his players. Those offbeat accents and jarring dissonances blew away many recording sessions and concerts than you could count. Call it jazz or call it great black music: it is more magnificent than you could describe. America should be grateful for its music royalty in Basie.

Count William Basie told me he wants to be remembered: "Just as I am right now...sittin' in front of a piano." I was a very humble human in the presence of William "Count" Basie, the kid from Redbank. Jeanette agreed, but we were never to see him again.

Tony Bennett before Westbury Concert.

Tony Bennett

The Other Saloon Singer
"HE'S FRISKY AND FRESH"

Tony Bennett credits all the old songwriters for his success. "It's not whether a song is new or old that makes it great...it's whether it's good or bad that makes them live or die."

He never gets tired of singing the worthy strains of Irving Berlin, Cole Porter, Harold Arlen, George Gershwin, or Harry Warren. He has a sort of instinct for selecting the songs that suit him. In the case of his immensely popular gem, *I Left My Heart in San Francisco,* he recalls that while rehearsing it with his piano accompanist, Ralph Sharon, in a Hot Springs hotel bar before he introduced it at the Fairmont Hotel in San Francisco, "A bartender was listening and, after we finished rehearsal, he told me he would *enthusiastically* buy a copy if we ever recorded it. That was the first tip-off that we had a hit in the making. Right up to today, it's my biggest request—it gets the best reaction, and San Francisco is really a beautiful city—it's a musical city—and I love to sing about it!" He doesn't seem to sing anything but the finest songs, although some argue that that song is considered too sentimental and weak, but it brings in the faithful and will probably be the song with which he will always be identified, happily or unhappily.

In 1983, Tony and I had a long talk backstage while Sarah Vaughan was singing on-stage and he was slated to follow. Tony is an excellent subject because he is eternally spirited about his music and his good luck, unlike the early struggles of Frankie Laine who was not discovered and finally appreciated until he was past thirty. Although their careers parallel, they do so more like ships passing in the night. Tony makes an art out of feelings: "I conjure up emotion much like impressionist artists who work with light. Feelings are the opposite of coldness...I try to sing in a natural key...choosing strong lyrics with meaning...then I inject my own feelings into it."

It's more than just feelings that drives Tony Bennett. Ever since he won an Arthur Godfrey Talent Scouts Contest (coming in second to Rosemary Clooney) Tony's career has always expanded upwards, helped along by a battery of million sellers, namely *Because of You, Rags to Riches, Blue Velvet,* (my, his mother's and Ella Fitzgerald's favorite*), Cold, Cold Heart, Boulevard Of Broken Dreams, I Left My Heart in San Francisco* and all those evergreens he has recorded over his career.

Bob Hope once told me that it was *he* that changed Tony's stage name of Joe Bari back to Tony Bennett (his real name is Anthony Dominick Benedetto) because *Bari* sounded phony. He had invited Tony to join his show at the New York Paramount after hearing him sing at Greenwich Village's Village Barn where he was appearing on the bill with Pearl Bailey. "Right there and then he announced what would be my new name and told me I was going on tour with him all over the U.S.—it was just great."

He loves to be associated with Sinatra, Armstrong, Ellington, and other greats of the swinging years... "Why between them they've written and played more music than anyone. They will go down in (music) history as being as important as Beethoven or Bach."

Tony considers his audiences *mature* and *civilized*, drawing a comparison to the sixties and seventies when rock & roll artists audiences were *not*. He also maintains he never really had a serious lull in his career: "I've always enjoyed long lines around the block where I opened, even during the Beatles invasion." We agreed that the rock and roll artists, in order to sustain a future for themselves that is consistent, must cross-over and satisfy new audiences with new product because those audiences mature and change too.

"Look at the new Linda Ronstadt ballad album," (arranged by the master, Nelson Riddle), he pointed out that evening in 1983, "It's a great album that has left her rock and roll albums in the dust...and is in the Top Ten *right now.*"

"With me, every show is my last show. When I had to record what record execs wanted back in the fifties, I did it and I luckily succeeded. But now I choose my own tunes to record with the help of my

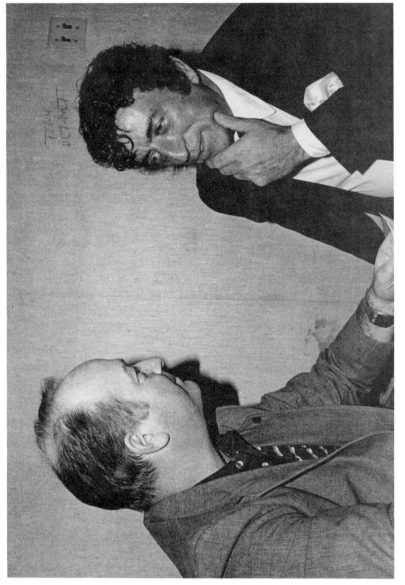

Tony Bennett recalls his early career.

longtime musical director and pianist, Ralph Sharon. I got some of those record executives angry when I wouldn't record some of the garbage they were peddling, so they called me a fanatic and a troublemaker. I consider it a *compliment*. They were forcing artists to take a dive. Remember, they're accountants and marketing guys, they don't know anything about the product. (That's exactly what Woody Herman complained about when I interviewed him.) When I come out to sing, I change and emotionalize and begin to feel the audience out there, and my songs come across more personalized—more sensitive—more dramatic—and I love it." He has matured into a more disciplined performer who communicates with his audience and never really ever sings a song the same way twice.

As a young man, Tony was trained to be a commercial artist at Manhattan's School of Industrial Arts, but he says, "I always had to sing, it was something in my genes...my Italian heritage—I have spent my whole life studying and thinking about singing...my whole family sang too!" He was influenced in those days by the school's choral director. He joined the chorus to learn his craft, and, after singing with military bands while serving in the armed forces in Europe, came home and entered the American Theater Wing professional school under it's director Miriam Spier. While studying, he rounded out a livelihood by playing club dates around Manhattan and even served as an elevator operator at the Park Sheraton Hotel to makes ends meet. That win on Talent Scouts led to a contract on a fifteen-minute, five-nights a week, radio show with Rosemary Clooney and eventually on Jan Murray's TV show, *Songs For Sale*.

Sinatra has said he owes his phrasing & breathing techniques to Tommy Dorsey's trombone playing, and Tony acknowledges that for him it was the instruction of both Art Tatum's piano and Mildred Bailey's jazz-voice. Sarah Vaughan described Tony Bennett to me one day as "...frisky and fresh. You've got to look at the movements in his face when he sings." she proclaimed. Sinatra, himself, also praises him: "He's my man, this cat, the greatest singer in the world today, Tony Bennett." And Bing Crosby, the original master popular singer, called him "the best singer in the business."

In 1978, Tony released two albums, one entitled *Tony Bennett and Bill Evans—Together Again* and *Tony Bennett Sings More Great*

Rodgers and Hart, both reaching fair success. In 1986 it was *The Art of Excellence* album. "Listen to this," he said from his dressing room in Atlantic City when the album came out and I called him to offer congratulations, "It's number one...and it's wonderful...and to think it's in front of the Rolling Stones and the great Bruce Springsteen. It's full circle for me." It was a good album containing an amazing duet with Ray Charles on James Taylor's *Everybody's Got the Blues* and a number called *City of Angels* which was written by Fred Astaire, plus my favorite of the album, an almost forgotten song from Irving Berlin's, Annie Get Your Gun, *I Got Lost in His Arms.* In 1993, he recorded an interesting album entitled, *Perfectly Frank,* which is a tribute to Frank Sinatra, but in the Bennett mold, and he won an Emmy for it. One *Time Magazine* critic said, "Moral: there are no definitive versions of great songs, only definitive singers." In 1994, he won an Emmy again, this time for a new album, *Steppin' Out,* which is a collection of Fred Astaire tunes.

"The thrill of performing hasn't changed in years. I learn something every day. I've never gotten bored yet and I don't think I ever will. It's funny...I mean I know it's hard to believe, but I'm 68 and, in my own mind, no matter what anybody else thinks, I feel I'm just starting out. I know now what I shouldn't do. And so, I feel as if I finally know what I can do and should do." He shakes his head and offers his famous, wide grin. "It's an amazing thing!"

It is amazing that this senior citizen appears regularly on MTV along with such artists as the perennial Eric Clapton and newcomer, Mariah Carey. "He's cool," say much younger fans. In 1995 he made numerous appearances including benefits for the Society of Singers and "unplugged" appearances on MTV Television and at Southampton College.

What's really amazing is that Tony also is another kind of artist— a landscape and portrait painter. He signs his works, *Benedetto* and sells them all over the world, (they go for from $6,000 to $40,000) which is also where he paints his subjects on canvas between shows while on tour, although lots of the paintings depict his children and grandchildren. Like many artists, he has painted a worthy portrait of himself. I saw some of his pieces one evening on display in the lobby of a theater where he was featured. They were mostly cityscapes and some landscapes. The portraits are fairly new to his work. From information gathered that evening with Tony, I was able to write a piece for an art magazine about his art alone.

Well, with his two new Grammy's to add to his others and his album total topping 90, he still walks on stage under Bob Hope's original advice: "Come out smiling, show the people you like them."

"To this day, I still follow that rule. Some performers say they don't care if the audience likes them or not. With that philosophy, they should stay home and do it."

Tony loves his life and his four kids, Danny, 42, Daegal, 39, Joanna, 25, and Antonia, 20. (The boys are in the music business with Danny, a former rock drummer, as his manager. I met him briefly after the show.) Tony is a modest man living the Zen philosophy. In his living room in mid-Manhattan, there is a Hirschfeld cartoon on the wall: The caption reads, *A group of America's Great Artists.*

"There's Ella, Bing Crosby, Nat King Cole, Fred Astaire, Judy Garland, and *I'm in that group.* I can't believe it, but it's true."

Yes, it's true, all right, and at his age, he looks and feels great. Besides MTV, at the Grammy's, singing on the Mall in Washington, D.C. on July 4th, you can find him anywhere the music is happening. He is more in focus now than he ever was. He appreciates his life, he is kind, and makes you feel good, whether friend or fan.

He will always keep going. He makes certain the interpretation of each song is exactly what he wants, and he surrounds himself with the best musicians he can find, regarding the interplay with them as important as his own delivery.

"Everyone thinks we keep him moving," says his one time bassist, John Burr, "but it is he who keeps us moving."

"When you first start painting, and it doesn't work out, you're devastated. But you keep painting. Then you're not bothered by your mistakes. You just say, 'The next time will be better.' That's what happens in life. That's why I wouldn't change anything: Because I made mistakes, but those mistakes taught me how to live, and boy, am I living."

Tony's latest album, *Here's to the Ladies*, is a grand excuse for him to perform some of Tin Pan Alley's best torch songs. Here's to you, Tony.

Talking with the golden voice of William B. Williams of WNEW.

Yapping with Billy Eckstine at Westbury Music Fair.

It's Make Believe Ballroom Time

Put All Your Care's Away
All the Bands Are Here to Bring Good Cheer Your Way

When Long Island's Westbury Music Fair announced that veteran radio disk jockey, William B. Williams, who hosted WNEW's quintessential music radio show, *The Make Believe Ballroom,* was going to emcee a nostalgic one-niter with singers Billy Eckstine, the smooth, sweet Margaret Whiting, and the exciting Glenn Miller Orchestra with current leader, Larry O'Brien, I promptly called William B., as he is affectionately known, at the Third Avenue studio and suggested a backstage interview with cast and guests backstage just before the show for *Long Island P.M. Magazine.* He loved the idea and, after clearing it with Westbury co-owner Lee Guber, we organized our interview cards and packed up our camera.

William B. had carried the torch some 30 years for the show, the keystone of the station's early success and once hosted by legendary *radio salesman* Martin Block. In-between, Jerry Marshall grabbed the helm in 1954 and William B. took over in 1963.

So, on November 5, 1983, photographer Camille Smith and I headed west from the hamlet of St. James on old Route 25-A to the beautiful, in-the-round, 2,800 seat theater originally built on Westbury's Brush Hollow Road as a summer stock tent in 1956, thirty feet below ground level. It was converted to a permanent building in 1966 with Jack Benny and Wayne Newton featured as headliners. We arrived at the stage entrance about an hour before show time.

William B. was an institution. I greatly admired his ability behind the microphone and his intimate knowledge of the music business. He was a *confidant* and trusted friend of Frank Sinatra, and was responsible for creating the Sinatra sobriquet, *Chairman of the Board.*

63

William B. or Willie B., as he liked being called, signed on every day at 10 A.M. with the droll greeting, *"Hello World!"* He was a professional in every sense of the word, admired and respected by the entire industry. WNEW, New York, was the flagship station for the Big Band Era and concurrently the music of Bing Crosby, Perry Como, Mel Torme, Nat "King" Cole, Tony Bennett, Kay Starr, the Andrew Sisters, Lena Horne, Ella Fitzgerald, and others of the same genre. William B. personally knew all the performers whose recordings he played on the show. They would frequently visit with him and exchange topics of the day, while he was on the air spinning their recordings:

"Bill, I know you enjoy doing the show, but how do you keep the patter going day after day and keep it fresh, interesting and lively?" I asked William B. when backstage with his son, Jeff, who was a pleasant young man all of 18, just visiting his dad at work.

"I think if somebody awakened me out of a truly deep sleep at 3 in the morning and put an on-air sign in front of me, I'd probably start talking automatically," drawled William B.

"There's a beauty to radio, in that the imagination comes into play. If I put on an old Miller, Sinatra, or Artie Shaw recording, people can close their eyes and take themselves back to a time when they first heard that recording. There is great therapy involved in getting out of stressful situations by listening to music associated with nicer days." He articulated so well. It must come from being aware of your voice-tones, pronunciations, and modulations after many years of practice and playbacks.

"The show was Westbury co-owner Lee Guber's idea," he went on, "he wanted to bring the show "live" to its thousands of fans. He felt they would make a good audience for the Big Bands and the singer—like Billy (Eckstine) and Margaret (Whiting))" William B. retained an impressive appearance with his silvery hair, good looks, and great stage presence.

We stepped into the rear dressing room where he introduced me to Billy Eckstine, one of those heroes I was telling you about whom I've admired over the years with those definitive renditions of *Caravan, I Apologize,* and *Everything I Have Is Yours.* But a little-known Eckstine ballad that I favored over all the others, entitled *Sitting By*

Dizzy visits Billy and me backstage at Westbury Music Fair.

the Window, was a wonderfully sad song that tugged at you, especially if you were a young man in love. I reminded Billy about it:

"The truth is, I was handed a lead sheet by a cabby one night after a show at the Copa. I figured it would be one of those "June, Moon, Spoon" things I would end up tossing, but I was wrong. An amateur wrote it and I ended up recording it and it went on to become a hit song for me. Haven't heard it much in the last thirty years." It was an Eckstine natural. It's now 1995 and *I* still can't locate a copy of it.

While B. (William B. simply called Eckstine 'B'), William B., and son Jeff were dressing, and we were recording and shooting the scene, jazz trumpeter, John Birks "Dizzy" Gillespie ambled in to the surprise of his old friends. He and Eckstine, of course, played together and were actually weaned in the Earl Hines Band of the early 40's, and later in Mr. B's own, short-lived band with fellow musicians Budd Johnson, Miles Davis, Charlie "Yardbird" Parker, Art Blakey, Fats Navarro and Gene Ammons. That conglomeration of talent was directly responsible for the birth of *Be-Bop*, the forerunner of what's now referred to as modern, cool jazz.

"Well, well! It's the *infamous* John Birks Gillespie, wanted in 50 states." declared Wm. B. almost triumphantly in those syrupy tones.

"And they haven't caught up to me yet." Dizzy retorted, laughing deeply and simultaneously greeting one and all, then flopping down on a convenient, comfortable couch, nesting his overcoat and fedora alongside as though he came to stay for a while.

"B, what about that thing you were telling me about... something about a rock-and-roll wife." William B. was plying Eckstine.

"Oh, yeah! I did one take on a thing called *Condemned to Life With A Rock And Roll Wife* and, John," he called to Diz, "my *momma* wouldn't even buy it." Gillespie almost fell off the couch laughing.

Mr. B. and Dizzy began swapping old musicians' war stories. There was one about a girl Dizzy met in New Orleans at the King of the Zulu's Parade, who said she came from a little town called Waycross, Georgia, and tantalizingly said to Dizzy: "Don't you remember me?" flaunting herself. Camille Smith, while shooting photos of the famous pair from every angle with both Nikon's, found himself irresistibly immersed in the roguish jokiness the two old friends had spontaneously spawned which had been a Gillespie trademark on and offstage over the years.

"When I hear about any kind of happening's in *Waycross*, Georgia, and *girls* are mentioned, *man*, I know that's a *line*," interrupted Camille Smith with some authority, unable to ignore what he was hearing.

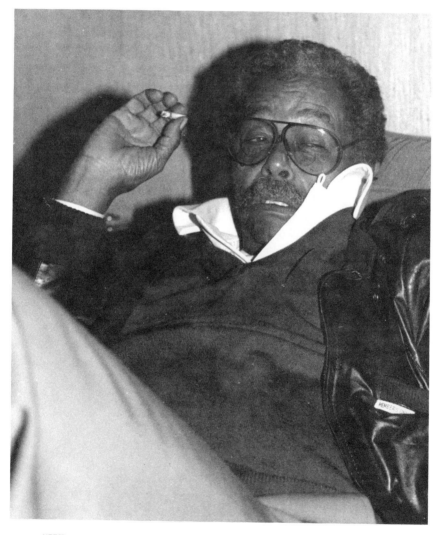

"Why are you bothering me" frowns a relaxing Billy Eckstine.

"Then you don't *know* what you're *talkin'* about." Mr. B. growled good naturedly at Camille.

"We were there many times. Isn't that right, John?" he said, looking at Dizzy. (Very few called Dizzy, John.) Then all three set to loudly challenging one another, contesting each others half-truths and bravados, and boasting of youthful deeds now recalled to discussion by aging comrades. Seldom have I witnessed such a degree of flagrant spouting, outright joy and laughter between old friends and one interloper. The laughter became contagious and William B. and I could not help but share their joy, although I wasn't really there. I wished I

Photographer and friend, Camille Smith.

68

could grasp their special language, but it was impossible, I was a square peg in a round hole.

There was something going on here that defied definition. Camille understood it all right, but later could not impart a clue of it into my northern brain. It was indeed rhetoric articulated by three mature black men, in a few spontaneous moments, that I failed to interpret. Here were two absolutely genuine icons of the Jazz Age, whose mark on music history is surely written in stone, simply being themselves.

Before our session was over, I asked Dizzy to recount the infamous bent trumpet story:

"Well, it was the result of an accident with an earlier trumpet. I threw a party for my wife back in the early 1950's and when I laid the trumpet down to get somethin' to eat, someone had stepped on it and bent it 90 degrees up. I didn't get too upset, though. (Now B was laughing.) It was a revelation of a sort. When I played it, I found that shape allowed the sound to reach my ear more quickly than before. It offered a better awareness of where the beat was, so now I bend all my trumpets." (Dizzy's trumpets are made custom for him with the upswept bell.) He put his finger to his lips and blew out his cheeks, then collapsed in laughter. "That's my other trademark!"

Dizzy is so well respected in the industry, (he even copped one of those Kennedy Center, Presidential medals the same night Katherine Hepburn received hers) mostly for his humanity, but also for his excellent skill and vision. Buddy Rich once told me he was Dizzy's number one fan:

"When you are as great as Diz—you're never satisfied with your playing. You try to improve upon it all the time. That's what makes him the greatest jazz trumpet in music. Like an architect you build and extend your work—that's what Diz means—you keep creating— you never stop."

The dressing rooms became gradually crowded the way they always do at such gatherings with well-wishers and staff, so Camille and I wandered out and across the corridor and into my favorite singer's dressing room and caught her primping in the mirror while trying on strings of pearls: "Hi Maggie," I said, to Margaret

69

Telling Margaret Whiting about *A Tree in the Meadows* great success.

Whiting, "You look great! I am always pleased to see you." I said to a solid kiss on the cheek.

Margaret's 1952 recording of *A Tree in the Meadow* was one of the longest running song hits played on the *Make Believe Ballroom*. She was only a teenager when she recorded it, and I was only a teenager when I played it to death on my new Admiral radio-phonograph back in Bay Ridge, Brooklyn. She sings lyrics like she believes every word, much like Frank Sinatra does. That's her success.

"Are you re-creating some of the great songs you've recorded on the show tonight?"

"Oh, Yes! I just came in from Midland, Texas, to do this show for Willie B., whom I love. I will do some of my father's songs—*My Ideal,* and *Till We Meet Again*, and some songs from my new album, *Speak Low*, and I am also doing *Moonlight in Vermont*" (a song that placed high on the all-time WNEW public poll taken in 1986). Maggie Whiting, daughter of Richard Whiting, the great song writer, grew up in a house where world-famous people like Al Jolson, Johnny Mercer, Judy Garland, Eddie Cantor, George Gershwin, Harold Arlen, and Jerome Kern were regular Saturday afternoon visitors.

"Growing up, I never knew anyone who wasn't famous," she recalled. Johnny Mercer, who was a close friend of her dad's, encouraged her and helped her make her first recording when he was head of Capitol Records. When her father died in 1938, Johnny Mercer became a sort of surrogate father to the very young Margaret. Under Johnny Mercer's guidance, she began recording and her first big hit was *That Old Black Magic* in 1942.

"But, what's going on here?" I asked. "Isn't our music supposed to be dead? Isn't rock and roll today's message?"

"It's a resurgence, we are *enjoying* a resurgence." she replied, "When I was touring for the last five years with 4 Girls 4, (an act with vocalists Helen O'Connell, Fran Warren, and Kay Starr) everyone was starving for our kind of music and we always sold out. People could have a choice. We could have gone on forever." At one point Rosemary Clooney and Rosemarie were members of that troupe. "We just got tired of all that traveling, all those years."

Margaret and I have exchanged many letters and notes over the years. I always send copies of articles I've written where she is a subject (like the Bob Hope USO tours which I often write about and in which she regularly participates or is even mentioned), or it may be a congratulatory note when she appears in Manhattan at the Algonquin Oak Room, Michael's Pub, or perhaps Freddy's Supper Club.

You must hear her version of *Slipping Around, (*an early crossover duet with Jimmy Wakely), *Come Rain Or Come Shine,* or *It Might As Well Be Spring,* which is also the name of her book co-authored with Will Holt. It was published in 1987 and went into an immediate second printing. It's no tell-all book, but it does provide a glimpse into her very privileged life as the daughter of an acclaimed songwriter

Listening to Maggie Whiting talk about "our kind of music."

and her own rise to become one of America's most respected song stylists.

We accompanied Margaret to the off-stage entrance ramp where she began warm-ups up by initiating small dance-steps and singing her selections acapella. Her cue came up and she skipped down the ramp to the stage where William B., the Glenn Miller Orchestra, and the audience was waiting.

Just before we left, Camille and I stood in the performers entrance wings catching the show through a curtain. We noticed Dizzy was standing in the aisle between sections with his overcoat on and his crumpled hat in clasped hands behind his back watching Mr. B sing. Two security guards who were standing alongside us began moving towards him and Camille and I nodded to one another with the unsaid thought that just maybe they intended to remove him from the aisle. Camille called to them and motioned them to return: "That guy I think you plan to toss out of here is Dizzy Gillespie who is visiting Billy Eckstine backstage." to their realization and relief. They thanked us: "We thought he was someone who sneaked in without paying." Camille just might have saved their jobs, who knows. He was mostly concerned that they didn't embarrass Diz or themselves.

"I feel like going on forever," Dizzy said some years later at his 75th birthday bash at New York's Bluenote in January 1992. But, as fate would have it, he was to leave us just one year later, only a few months after he actually reached the age of 75. Mr. B went just before him and William B. even before that in 1986. Where is everybody going?

I was to work once again with William B. Williams a year after this occasion in 1984 doing the same gig but this time with my friend, Frankie Laine; perky, frisky, Helen O'Connell, and teddy bear, Buddy Morrow who was leading the Tommy Dorsey ghost band and whose real name was Moe Zudicoff. William B. was already beginning to feel the pain cancer began dealing him.

After William B. passed on in 1986, I received this note from Maggie:

"...remember our meeting at Westbury a few seasons ago with William B. God, I miss him—as a friend—but, most of all, I miss him on the air. WNEW just isn't the same any more. I know they're trying,

73

but when Willie died and they let Bob Jones and Jim Lowe go, the whole kind of programming they used to do is just gone." It got worse. WNEW went *off the air* December 2, 1992. The great voice was still.

Now, in 1995, most of those voices, including Jonathon Schwarz and Bob Jones are on the air again. New York radio station WQEW was organized a year before and great music is being heard again. Margaret Whiting and I are greatly relieved. Our music is back playing in New York.

Westbury Music Fair Front Marqueé, 1983.

75

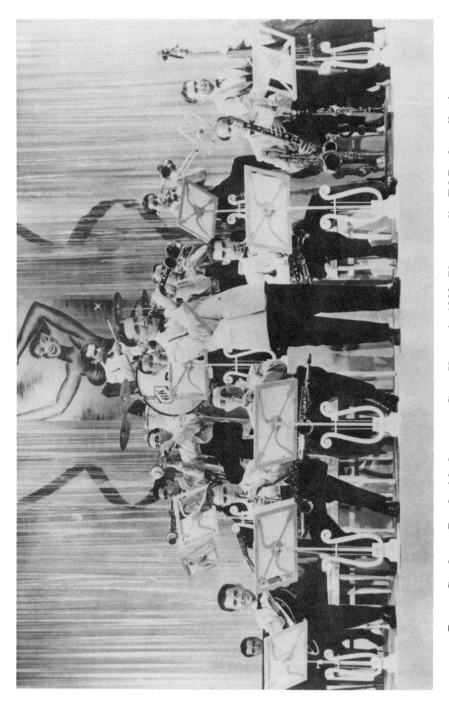

Benny Goodman Band with drummer Gene Krupa in 1939. Photo credit: Ed Burke collection.

Benny Goodman Day

THE KING OF SWING VISITS LONG ISLAND
His real voice was his clarinet.

The King is dead. Long Live the King. But there would be no other king in this case. For over 50 years Benny Goodman was the *King of Swing,* securely anchored to his musical throne since that one night in 1934 when he almost single handedly ushered in the Swing Era only moments after his smashing and triumphant success at Los Angeles' Palomar Ballroom. "I called out for one of our big Fletcher Henderson arrangements," he remembered, "and the boys seemed to get the idea." The crowd stopped dancing and rushed the bandstand. The rest of the story you'll find in the public library under *Jazz History.*

And, indeed, it was Benny Goodman who brought needed respectability to jazz with an absolutely all-star ensemble at his milestone 1938 Carnegie Hall concert that shaped music history and opened the doors forever to every jazz musician who would follow. A generation was mesmerized by the sound of his master instrument and incomparable style.

In 1982, when Jack Ellsworth of radio station WLIM invited me to "Benny Goodman Day," I was elated. It was, at last, my chance to talk to him. Benny was to be chauffeured by limousine to North Patchogue in central Long Island. Jack, who interviewed Benny many years before in Providence, R.I. and maintained a relationship with him over the years, secretly confided to me that Benny absentmindedly believed Jack was once his manager and so he agreed to come out to be a guest on Jack's popular "Memories in Melody" show. Jack would play his records all day long and Benny would meet the station's advertisers, friends, and local dignitaries and be interviewed by me and NBC Television's 6:00 o'clock News team. It was an absolute

77

WLIM's Jack Ellsworth and his son welcome Benny Goodman.

grand slam for Jack who had just started up his radio station a few months before, lending a needed boost to his eventual success over his former employer, another local station who was now his main competition.

So, without entouragé or fanfare, without bodyguard or secretary, without agent or impresario, Benny Goodman arrived in a late-model station wagon at WLIM's tiny, white-washed building with its two, very tall and narrow, fenced-in antennas hovering nearby, where I greeted him along with Jack's wife, Dorothy, and photographer, Camille Smith, who took most of the photos in this book. Benny's first words were: "Where the hell am I?" uttered in a somewhat tired, gravelly voice and with a wry smile.

"Welcome to North Patchogue," said I, happily shaking his distinctive dead-fish, unenthusiastic hand. A lone, older fan stood anxiously on the sidelines hoping for an autograph. Benny spotted him and graciously signed his name, uttered a few kind words, and then walked into the building with that slow gait and quizzical grin.

Jack was "On-the-air" in the tiny studio. Bob Dorian, WLIM's morning man, now famous interviewer and host in his own right on "American Movie Classics" channel on cable television, helped us guide our "King" into Jack's office, the largest room in the small building. He directed him to a comfortable couch situated under a large, colorful banner boasting the station's call letters near where Dorothy had set up a neat paper-plate deli lunch on a folding table covered with a large, disposable tablecloth. Benny grabbed a pastrami sandwich while being introduced to station personnel, valued advertisers, and local dignitaries.

By that time the NBC crew had arrived and began plying their trade, but Camille Smith was able to hold them back until my interview with Benny was complete. Benny and I sat face to face on the couch and talked about Lionel Hampton, Teddy Wilson, and Gene Krupa, his famous sidemen of the Benny Goodman Quartet. Surprisingly, I could tell that Benny was feeling a bit bewildered. Was this the giant who brought that wonderful swing-music into the lives of countless millions? Is this the man who broke the color line in music by bringing the great jazz-pianist Teddy Wilson and Lionel Hampton

79

With Benny Goodman at WLIM talking about the Bluebird Years.

into an all-white band before a startled public? There was no doubt about those facts.

Our conversation centered around his affection for the old "Bluebird" series recordings which he favors over all his other work. He recalled that it was Gene Krupa, his favorite drummer, who coined the words *Swing Band* one day while touring in Colorado in response to a reporter's inquiry about their new style of music. "We just call it *swing!*" said Krupa.

Minutes later, Jack was ready for his on-the-air interview where he and Benny introduced and played various recordings. At one point while they were on live, Jack asked him: "Benny, how do you feel about a full day of your music on our station?" And Benny shot back: "Well, if you can take it—so can I," to everyone's laughter.

And later when we asked him if there were any new mountains he wanted to climb, or if there was anything he hadn't done that he would like to do, he smiled and said: "I think I did it today. Coming here was quite a trip. I thought we'd never get here," he added, uncharacteristically, to almost uncontrollable laughter. Benny still thought he was some sixty miles further out in Montauk Point at the eastern end of Long Island.

Later, while carefully sipping coffee, Benny didn't notice the awe in the faces of some as they politely took turns sitting very close beside him while someone clicked a camera. I'm sure he did not notice the reactions, the undercurrent or the daring it must have required to approach him or maybe ask for an autograph without compromising their own professionalism. Some wanted to talk with him—but what would they say? It seemed too unreal that here, on this very spot, at this very moment, was seated one of the great icons of the century, a man who is assured a place in music history, and in a moment or two he would be gone from them perhaps forever.

He was the genuine article, the epitome of what the entire radio station represented musically from morning till night every day of the year, much like hundreds of similar stations throughout the country.

In an unexpected moment I sensed Benny's patience was waning and he signaled accordingly by excusing himself and backing out the door into an anteroom in preparation for his leaving. "Get me out of here," he growled, "I'm tired." He clearly needed to leave; good-

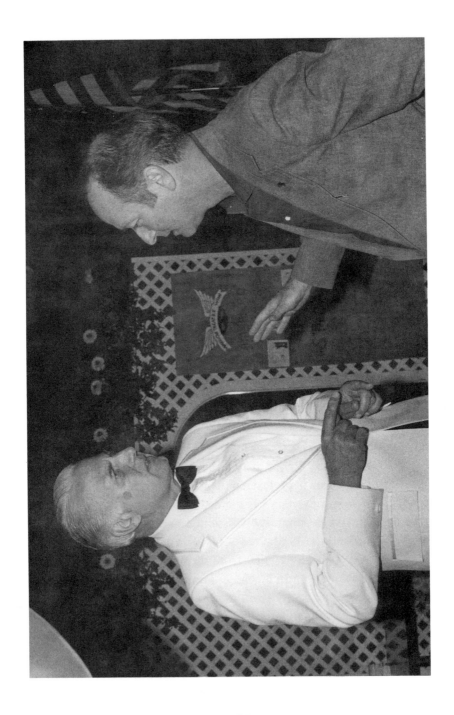

byes and vows were quickly exchanged and we guided him into the station wagon in just about the same way he arrived.

The station buzzed for days afterwards and there was a glow all over the village. Jack Ellsworth walked taller, his enthusiasm reinforced, his purpose justified. I beam still to this day, some 12 years later, for as a chronicler of such individuals, it was an all-important day: my personal audience with the "King."

Benny Goodman passed away from us on Friday, June 13, 1986; and in 1989, his daughter, Rachel Goodman Edelson, who was engaged at the time writing a documentary about her father's life, wrote to me about the progress of her book and enclosed a booklet and an actual clarinet reed once used by her father. He used to throw them on the floor and she gathered them daily and collected them, when he rehearsed in his studio at home on East 66th Street in New York City. It was a welcome present—a personal link.

Benny Goodman has thrilled generations with his exciting, pulsating, uncompromising improvisations on his master instrument, the swinging clarinet. To sum it up, George T. Simon, author of the book *The Big Bands,* once wrote, "How many other Kings, musical or regal, have done as much for so many of us for so many years?"

Richard Grudens and friend Bob Hope talk about Bing Crosby.

Bing Crosby's Musical Legacy

Hey Son! Can I Use the Phone?

It was in 1952 when I first met Harry Lillis Crosby. He was my mother's favorite crooner. All throughout my young life, it was *Where the Blue of the Night Meets the Gold of the Day,* or *Come to Me My Melancholy Baby,* and, *I Found A Million Dollar Baby in A Five & Ten Cents Store.*

Working the sixth-floor desk as a radio and television studio page for NBC in Rockefeller Center, New York, you were accustomed to world-famous celebrities coming and going about all day. One moment you were working the Texaco Star Theater with television mega-star, Milton Berle, known at that time as "Mr. Television," and his countless celebrity guests; the next day it may have been apportioning the seats in Studio 6A while the great contralto, Marion Anderson or the Italian basso, Ezio Pinza, star of Rodgers and Hammerstein's *South Pacific,* was rehearsing with Donald Vorhees and the Bell Telephone Orchestra.

You went about your business.

However, when I spotted crooner Bing Crosby talking to movie star Robert Montgomery (father of Elizabeth Montgomery), my chest collided with my stomach, and my mother's face, singing one of those songs, appeared in my mind's eye. It was *HIM!* Maybe that's the way some fans of Frank Sinatra or Elvis Presley felt at that special moment.

He sauntered over to my desk and parked his butt on the corner and scooped up the phone inquiring: "Hey, son! Can I use the phone?" "Sure," I shot back. He did and after a moment or two he was heading for the elevator bank and I watched him fade out of my life. However, at the time, my interest in him consisted only of telling mom that I met *her* hero. It was only many years later that my interests in him elevated as I became a chronicler of him and all the participating players who generated the wonderful music of the Jazz Age. Since that day, and as a member of the Bing Crosby Historical Society, and later of the Bingthings Society, I have woefully regretted not seizing that opportune moment by pervading the ninth floor with questions to one of the principal musical performers of the century.

Well, I missed the boat! But, who knew? And to further realize that I was stationed on the fifth floor desk at least twice a week for over 6 months during the same period of time while Paul Whiteman, Bing's former employer and leader of the biggest jazz orchestra of the thirties and known as "The King of Jazz," walked by my desk and cordially waved to me before entering his office almost every day. I let that opportunity go by too.

Paul Whiteman's most famous employee, Bing Crosby, indeed, became *the* pioneer vocalist, the ground-breaker, who paved the way for Perry Como, Frankie Laine, Mel Torme, Tony Bennett, Dean Martin, Elvis Presley, Pat Boone, yes, and even Frank Sinatra, who emulated Bing even to wearing a hat and smoking a pipe like Bing used to do.

It was Bing's musical legacy. And they all acknowledge it in one way or another. Unlike the voices of the early innovators, song-belter Al Jolson or the operatic-sounding John McCormack, Laurence Tibbett and Nelson Eddy, and the limp-stylists, collegiate vocalist and band-leader, Rudy Vallee and Gene Austin (*Ramona*), Bing set aside the half-notes and quarter-notes and instead infused meaning and empathy into every word. In doing this, he personalized the delivery by omitting artistic pretensions, thus shifting the focus of the song so it would exist only between him and the listener. He arrived on the music scene precisely at the right time, making all the right stylistic moves. He became the first singer to make the new kind of microphones work to his favor while keeping the song going.

"I'm not a singer; I'm a phraser," Bing once said, "that means that I don't think of a song in terms of notes; I try to think of what it purports to say lyrically. That way it sounds more natural and anything more natural is more listenable."

Bing inadvertently became the catalyst for launching the careers of hundreds of singers who came after him because he was the

Frank Sinatra and Bing in *High Society*.

accepted sound from 1925 through the Big Band Era, even stretching into the late 60's. By his own admission he was the first popular singer who interpreted the lyrics of a song and then phrased each line carefully to make it sound believable.

"He was my hero, the father of my career. All that mattered to him was the words," said Frank Sinatra. Frank's recording of *Ciribiribin* with Harry James proves all of this in no uncertain terms. Frankie Laine revealed that he was also strongly influenced by Bing's great sounds of success. "I used to imitate Bing perfectly during Marathon Dancing Days, especially with the songs *Straight From the Shoulder* and *Soon."*

Perry Como acknowledges that he tried to sing *I Surrender Dear* and *Temptation* just as Bing did earlier in his 1931 recordings. Some of Perry's recordings sound so much like Bing that you have to listen very carefully to distinguish them. Perry's *Prisoner of Love* and *Till the End of Time* are clearly sprinkled with Bing's crooning style.

Pull out your copy of Dean Martin singing *Wrap Your Troubles in Dreams,* Bing's original 1931 gem, or *Love Is Just Around the Corner* and *Sweet and Lovely* (a real trademark Crosby song) and you will see what I mean. They could be classified as almost an impression. Listen carefully to his version of *Goodnight Sweetheart.*

And Pat Boone's recordings of *Love Letters in the Sand* and *Gold Mine in the Sky* are open acknowledgments by Pat himself of his conscious imitation of Bing as a stepping stone to success. Pat is honored when any comparison is made between him and Bing. All that was missing was the deeper baritone vibrato.

Tony Bennett told me that as a young man he, too, was influenced by Bing's way with a ballad. He liked the casual way he presented his songs: "He made it look and sound easy. Bing's relaxed style made me more and more interested in music. He has actually molded American music and infused jazz and style in the highest quality, especially his collaborations with Louis Armstrong."

When Elvis crooned *Love Me Tender* or *Can't Help Falling in Love With You*, you hear unmistakable traces of Bing's style. Elvis openly admitted his indebtedness and admiration of Bing Crosby.

Bing always admired his fellow performers and teamed up with almost every known vocalist of his time. From Al Jolson to Fred

Astaire to non-singers Bob Hope, Grace Kelly, and trombonist, Jack Teagarden, from the Andrew Sisters to the Mills Brothers, he helped make great competitors of them all.

Boy, am I sorry I didn't think about all this before that fateful day I missed the boat on Bing! However, when I interviewed Bob Hope in 1984, we talked in depth about his former sidekick. Here's what Bob had to say about his versatile movie partner.

"Bing was definitely the best of the singers of my day. He was one of those rare people who supported a comedian, too. He had an awareness of others' needs, professionally and otherwise. He and I would ad-lib on the set and the director would keep it in like it was written for us. Bing got along with everyone and he moved his fellow performers along—he was a great straight man. Bing and I had a special kind of chemistry—and when I would sing along with him in the 'Road' pictures, he would never try to upstage me, or sing above me, even though I found it hard to carry a tune. We were two people, two different personalities that fit—just like that. God knows where that came from."

As a footnote, however, in 1992 thanks to Bob Lundberg, President of the Bingthings Society of Tacoma, Washington, I was gratified to acquire a remarkable collection of Bing Crosby video tapes. These five tapes, each two hours long, contain all Bing's songs chronologically from his films, beginning with *The King of Jazz* (with Paul Whiteman's Orchestra) in 1930, through *Robin & The Seven Hoods* in 1964 and every film between—even those considered *shorts*, or cameo roles. As long as there was a song sung by Bing in a film, it was on the tapes. The format: opening and titles, the songs, then closing credits. The film, *Holiday Inn*, contains thirteen, including duets with Astaire, others just one or two. So every evening can be a special evening watching and listening, yes...welcoming the master of them all. As Henry Pleasants observed in his book *The Great American Popular Singers;* "When we hear Bing Crosby, we recognize the voice of an old and treasured friend."

With Buddy Rich in his band bus, 1982.

Buddy Rich

Grandstanding Drum Wonderboy

Upon casual inquiry, everyone who is anyone counseled against pursuing an interview with big band music bad boy, Buddy Rich. They said it wouldn't work. Big Band writer and broadcaster, Don Kennedy, of *Big Band Jump* radio fame said: I once did a quickie (interview) but didn't get nearly anywhere; he was most difficult (with me)...maybe a (another) clash of personalities." Buddy clashed with many and often.

Tony Bennett actually shook his head and shrugged his shoulders about such a possibility: "He's a tough one. He doesn't like it. Buddy keeps to himself in the bus." A large Band bus is parked outside the theater where he "lives" during tours. He almost never uses backstage theater dressing rooms.

They said he was arrogant, sharped-tongued, downright nasty. But Mel Tormé was his friend, and Mel Tormé talked with him often and they got along well. Two opposites.

However, one lucky night after some lovely conversation with the enchanting and sweet Sarah Vaughan between shows, we spotted Buddy Rich's band bus out of view in a rear parking lot. It was a bitter 10 degree winter evening and very windy in the lot. It appeared like a spaceship just waiting to aspire upwards into the firmament. With steam rising from above the craft, photographer Camille Smith and I wandered over and simply rapped on the door a few times. A young man opened the door and asked what we wanted. We explained our circumstances and produced our card. He nodded for us to wait and flipped the door closed (we thought we could hear the theme from the *Twilight Zone* riding the bitter winds), but in a moment Buddy Rich appeared perky and fresh from a shower wrapped in a terry-cloth robe and a brand new New York Yankees baseball cap. He posed the same question, and we replied accordingly. "All right—" he held his finger high like teacher to truant student and said, "I'll give you two minutes." But it was said with a mischievous smile or was it an impatient grin? We were admitted.

Brooklyn born all-time ace drummer, Bernard Rich talked his head off that cold winter evening, which we now know was a rarity, so I thought it best to print it just the way I asked it and he answered it. Talking came easy to him. He's played with them all, beginning with his first recording as back-up drummer on the Andrew Sisters' evergreen, *Bie Mir Bist Du Shoen*. As you will be able to determine from the next few pages, Buddy is bright, witty, and very, very smart. His acid wit was always in evidence:

RG: Buddy, people in the trade say you are the busiest and most traveled band leader on the scene today. We recently talked to Woody Herman who says he hates the traveling, but loves the music.

BR: Well, if I didn't like it, I wouldn't do it. I like to enjoy my life. I certainly prefer this to getting in a car and driving up and down expressways going to an office all day—the traffic is insanity—to me this is an absolutely normal way of life—it's perfect. I see the whole world, man! (pause) Who could do better than that?

RG: How have you been feeling since your illness? (His 1983 bypass operation.)

BR: I never think about it. I never really think about it.

RG: People say, of course they'll always talk, that you drive yourself hard, you play (the drums) hard, and you work even harder.

BR:...and I live hard! I also hold a black belt in martial arts. I'm in good shape. I don't think I drive myself hard. I do what my body tells me to do and I never go any farther than what my body says.

RG: Recently I talked to Johnny Mince. You remember Johnny from the Dorsey days (an excellent clarinetist profiled in this book) I asked him about your fights with Frank Sinatra where you would throw things at each other...what interests me (I had to talk fast, as this made him uncomfortable) is how you got back together again. What happened there? When did it end?

BR: The next day. You see, when you're twenty-two years old and you're both striving for a certain amount of recognition, after all I was a sideman in the band and he was the singer, we both wanted to be recognized and both trying to do something, you have ego problems. Then you grow up and realize that ego is bullshit. It's what you do and be recognized for that counts. You have to become friends. You just can't carry on a vendetta—it's insanity. We're friends, of course we're friends. We've been friends for years.

RG: Is that legendary story true about you sending up a fan to ask Frank (Sinatra) for a number of autographs and he told Frank that he would trade in four of his for one of Bob Eberly (singer with Jimmy Dorsey who made those wonderful duet recordings with Helen O'Connell).

BR: That's the most bullshit story that ever was told. It never happened. My mind doesn't work in that area, and I like to think of myself as a fairly witty person. I don't have to go around doing bad moves and bad numbers on people. I'd rather do it with my so-called brain than have to resort to childish bullshit things. So that story, I must have heard it a million times in the last thirty years, and to sit and deny it only makes it more feasible, so I don't talk about it at all...so I just finished doing five minutes on it. (loud laughter from Buddy, Camille, and myself.)

RG: Buddy, it is true that you taught yourself to play the drums?

BR: I don't know if I've ever taught myself. I've never taken a lesson, if that's what you mean. You can't teach yourself something unless you know it first. So I think I just did it. I had a natural ability, I guess.

RG: Who do you look up to in your own field?

BR: From the time I was able to recognize the talents of various drummers from the early thirties until the present day, I've been impressed with everybody that has ever played. Every body you listen to leaves some kind of mark on your brain and on your ear and there are things you dislike and things you love. I happen to be a lucky guy because I came up at the time where there were fifty great drummers. Besides Krupa there was Chick Webb, Jo Jones, and I could go on and name you names like Sid Catlett, Davey Tough, Spencer O'Neil, and people you probably never heard of each of whom impressed me, of course! And I was friends with all those guys.

RG: I guess you played a lot with Krupa in the past.

BR: Gene and I did tours with Jazz at the Philharmonic for six years.

RG: Was that the (Norman) Granz thing?

BR: Yeah, Norman Granz.

RG: Who books all your work now, Willard?

BR: Yes, Willard Alexander and his agency in New York.

RG: Dizzy Gillespie told me, not too long ago, that everything he does he wants to extend further. Like an architect who puts up a building and adds on to it. He extends his work and his work grows, so someday he can be looked to as somebody who always improved in his work. Do you have any comment on that? Is that your way too?

BR: You see, it would be a very biased comment because I'm such a fan of Diz. For him to say that is only a natural extension of how he feels about life. His playing—when you are as great as Diz— you're never satisfied with your playing. You try to improve upon it all the time. That's what makes him the greatest jazz trumpet in music. That's what he means—you're just creating—you never stop.

RG: We were just talking to Tony Bennett a few days ago, and he says when he gets in front of an audience his emotions rise and he becomes another person on stage. He thinks that's why people are attracted to him. This is why they come to see him perform. Now, when you're on stage you are Buddy Rich the performer, and here you are Buddy Rich the man. Do you feel any kind of high or emotion when you are on stage?

BR: When I'm on stage. I'm Buddy Rich—the Buddy Rich.

RG: Are you saying you're the same on or off?

BR: I involve myself in my playing and I involve myself with my band and become one with the audience. It isn't a separate thing. There's an energy level when people listen and understand what you're doing and you become one thing—the energy goes from them to us—from us to them. I don't feel any difference when I'm around people who give me the same kind of energy feeling. That is on the stage or off. There's an emotional impact somewhere.

RG: Buddy, someday there will be somebody like me who will write the history of this kind of music—maybe twenty-five years down the road. How will you want the world to see Buddy Rich of these days?

BR: As I am!

RG: Tell me what that is.

BR: Well, I'm a million things. Tell me what you are! You can't—you see. To be able to say what you are—you are many things to many different people. You just got through saying that Tony Bennett feels he's a different person when he's on stage—another personality. I, too, have many personalities. I'm funny. I'm arrogant. I'm sad. I'm angry. I'm all the emotions that you can have in a body. I am, so to say, what kind of a guy are you?—well, I'm the same kind of guy you are. You're unhappy when something sad happens and happy when you feel good, and you're good when you feel happy. You're in love, out of love. You eat and don't eat, and all the things you are—you are. *That's you.* That's what I am. I don't say who I am. It's what I am. I'm a whole lot of things. People misunderstand me. They think, "Well this guy, you can't talk to him. He's this and he's that." O.K. That's the personality he sees. That's how he'll remember me. No matter what I do he'll remember me as being an arrogant S.O.B. "Who does he think he is?"

Somebody else will see me as a fairly sensitive man who understands a whole lot of things and though others will fight about it. "He's not really like that,"...and so...who are you?

RG: Changing subjects—Benny Goodman recently told me he thinks the musics are merging—crossing over—that people are dancing again. Any comment? What's happening to the music business?

BR: *How the hell do I know?* (laughing mischievously)

RG: You're in the business. You are supposed to know these things. (I was scolding him/chiding him.)

BR: Well, anything that Benny Goodman says has some basis of truth because to me he's the greatest thing that ever happened to jazz. From the beginning since I heard his band in 1936. I remember vividly the first time I heard it, up until that time I used to listen to the radio to the old Casa Loma, Glen Gray Band and I thought that was the hottest thing that ever happened until I heard Goodman's band. And I went WHOA! I was 16 years old then...what the hell's that all about? I mean it was another thing entirely. I grew on Benny's music and I am a great fan of his. I love him—he's nuts—but I love him.

RG: Of all the recordings done by all the big bands, including your own, which one do you rate the best?

BR: None.

RG: What does that mean?

BR: The kinds of things I listen to you would not think somebody like me would listen to. I like the old Jackie Gleason things with Bobby Hackett on the trumpet. I am a great fan of good singers—Sinatra, Torme, Bennett, Jack Jones, Eckstine—people like that. So, instead of listening to every hot jazz group that comes along, I'm selective about that. But, I happen to like, and this is not a step back, this is not nostalgia, this is music to my ears, instead of the junk screaming and yelling to loud guitars—the only way to get back to reality is to listen to someone where a guy wrote a lyric about something besides getting laid by some broad. He wrote about love and there was a story for 32 bars and a musical concept and arrangements and loveliness. So that's what I listen to. It's not your favorite recording—it's your overall favorite music. All good music is my favorite. I hate bad stuff.

RG: And our last question Mr. Rich is—simple and silly though it may seem, but they draw you out. Who is your favorite musician, living or not living, in this business as we know it?

BR: That's an impossible question to answer because there are so many great artists you just can't pick out. I often get asked, "What is the perfect All Star band?" There will never be an All-Star band until you put every star that ever played together. You can't say one thing about one guy because there's, also, that other guy that you love. So you can't say who's your favorite because there are too many of them—like the great Count Basie band, Ellington's band, Woody's old bands, Goodman...it's just impossible to say. I love Stan Getz (musing) and I love Coleman Hawkins, Lester Young, and Ben Webster. So you can't insult the other giants. So all of them are my favorites.

EPILOGUE

Well, we did it! And afterwards, Buddy said, "I told you five minutes and I've given you forty minutes. How the hell did I do that?"

For the first time I realized that all along he was trying to justify all of that to us. That some people have type-cast him as the *heavy*. But he was explaining that he really was a mis-understood guy with an undeserved reputation, but with a brisk personality that has been mistaken for gruffness and arrogance. Why even some of our inquiries involved that question. He was informing us he was an O.K. kind of guy after all, and that it was okay to get together and talk. He was blunt and definite, and it was difficult to argue with his rational philosophy, his kindnesses to fellow performers, and the personal praise of his own heroes. Some peers said he was too demanding and a mercurial leader, expecting excellence from other musicians with respect to timing and execution. Some were intimidated by those sharp criticisms, but all agreed his musical performances were beyond reproach.

Buddy Rich's performances occupied the extremes of American entertainment—and his musical approach was indeed a reflection of his personality. He was aggressive one moment and sentimental the next. The latter was how we saw him that day.

A brain tumor took Rich away at the age of 69. He was brave in the face of this illness right up to the end.

Kay Starr romps at Huntington, Long Island, Concert.

Kathryn La Verne Starks
Native American

"You Can Feel the Memories Starting"

On the drive to the (Harry) Chapin Rainbow Stage in Huntington's Heckscher Park to meet Kathryn La Verne Starks, a.k.a. Kay
Starr, I stuffed a re-issued Glenn Miller album which included the little-known numbers *Baby Me* and *Love With A Capital You* in the car
tape deck and let play them over and over, listening carefully to those
very sweet Miller evergreens and the light and fluffy female delivery.
Both featured Kay Starr on the vocal. She was just a mere fifteen then
and had recorded these two sides for the Miller band because their
regular girl singer, Marion Hutton, was ill. It wasn't the *Wheel Of
Fortune* Kay Starr you would easily recognize; it was the pre-Charlie
Barnet-who-would-change-her voice-forever-era-Kay Starr, but it was
definitely the best female vocalizing ever heard on a Miller recording,
although there were only a few recognizable traces of the legendary
vocalist we all know so well.

When Marion returned the next week, "Mom and I packed our
bags and got back home to Memphis with just three cents in our
pocket."

She was nine years old when she first sang on a Dallas, Texas
radio station. "It was on WRR at the Melba Theater in Dallas."

"And for no pay." I documented, prying easily.

"Right—no pay!"(girlish laughter).

"A fifteen minute show for five days a week."

"Yes, then much later when I was fourteen, I went with Joe Venuti and was with him every summer 'til I was sixteen...then briefly
with Glenn Miller where I made those two recordings." I told her of
my musical homework during my trip to the theater.

"Your voice was so different. I learned somewhere that you had (voice) trouble when you were with Charlie Barnet."

"I did, after singing for three years with Charlie, and you're singing over George Serabo's arrangements, you can bet that it affected my throat. It actually ruined my voice temporarily...a lot of people said that it made me sound different...the keys didn't change, so...I don't know."

"Well, maybe it was just a change over the teen-age sound."

"It could be, but you know it took me a year to recover and I started with piano and they let me add bass after many weeks then drums with no sticks, just brushes, for more weeks and it took me all that time before I was able to sing with a full-blown band again. I had to learn everything all over again like having to walk from a crawl." She was thinking it over, not having talked about it much lately, she said.

"So the loud Barnet band *was* indirectly responsible."

"Partially. I think that ignorance is bliss. Charlie would say, 'So your throat's bad. So what...sing anyway. '...and I listened to him like an idiot."

I recounted that Patty Andrews told me much the same thing happened to her and she had to have re-training, which she says helped her career because she learned to breathe better and was able to avoid the problems of strain.

"I sang over, around and under colds the whole time I was with Barnet, but then I finally developed a sort of pneumonia and was on the verge of (throat) polyps, and I'm sort of a frontier woman, I don't get sick easily or stay sick very long and it was not my nature to faint, but I did for the first and only time in my life. Even on those Miller recordings you just mentioned, I wanted to make those records so badly that I sang above my key...again...Marion sang one-and-a-half octaves higher than I...but I did it anyway, it made no difference."

Was she nervous at that tender age? "No, I was excited. I was so young."

Some say that after all that throat trouble she developed a huskier, throaty voice, which is really her trademark, the sound that unmistakably identifies her.

"Well, maybe..." She gives in a little... "maybe I just grew up."

While with Joe Venuti and the Camel Caravan show, Kay left to get back to Tech High in Memphis. "I thought Joe was trying to get rid of me, so I cried. It was a panic." But Joe finally got her to understand that he really liked her and that she had to finish school then she would be able to go to Detroit and then to New York with the band to do a radio show.

Next, it was work with Bing's brother, Bob Crosby. As his vocalist, she was approached by the Camel Cigarettes people to star in a weekly radio show, but the deal fell through. "The ad agency wanted a bigger name." she said.

Of all the familiar, successful songs she recorded with Capitol during her career, including *Side-By-Side, Bonaparte's Retreat, Angry,* and her golden *Wheel of Fortune,* she names the latter as her favorite and claims never to get tired of singing it. "When I think I'm wearied of it, and I wonder, Oh, maybe people are tired of it. But what happens is, every time I start to sing it, somebody reaches over and touches somebody next to them, or they just smile, and you can just feel the memories starting, you know, and you can't deny that's what it's all about."

"It was like the marriage between Tony Bennett and *I Left My Heart in San Francisco* and Frankie Laine with *I Believe.*"

"Yes, and the people love it the best. And, don't forget, it bought me my house and determined my future."

Wheel of Fortune has sold over 5 million records and was just beginning to sell in Russia.

In the seventies Kay took her act to Lake Tahoe and Las Vegas, working about 25-30 weeks a year at places mostly of her own choosing and singing a repertoire of her own choice.

"You once said that a good singer is a singer who tells a story to music. Do you stand by that statement today?"

"Well, actually what I said was, a singer is no more than an actor or actress set to music, because you are only as good as the story you tell and people like to hear things they can identify with, and *that's* the *story.*"

When we tried to cover the ground of who she considered to be the best of her counterparts, she wound up with an interesting viewpoint with respect to other vocalists: "To be perfectly honest, I like

101

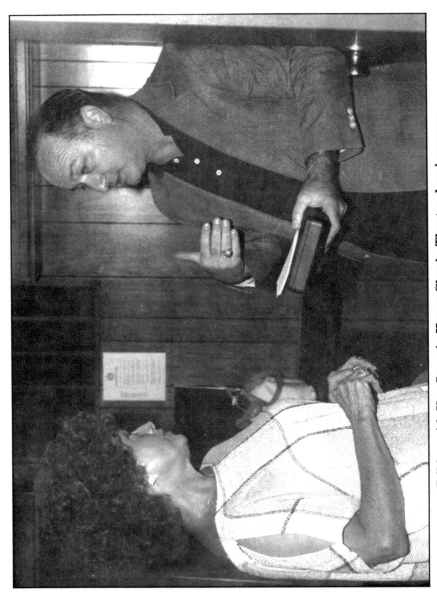

Talking with Kay Starr in Harry Chapin Theater dressing room.

different singers for different reasons. Sometimes I like them because they have a nice sound, and sometimes because they can deliver a lyric pretty good...and there's lots of them...but, I think I like the guys better than the gals...but...no one special."

Kay Starr started out in "Country." Being from Oklahoma and composed of ¾ Cherokee and ¼ Irish blood, it was a natural progression.

"I was a child of the Depression and we didn't have any money to buy records, we didn't have a record player, so whoever was big on radio, I listened to. I lived in Texas—that's country music territory."

Through the fifties she sang what is now her world-famous repertoire, and in the sixties she went back to "Country" ("didn't everyone, and it was natural for me to do it, it being my roots"). The seventies saw a little of both, and two albums, *Kay Starr Country* and *Back to the Roots*. In the eighties it was a nationwide tour with Four Girls Four (Margaret Whiting, Helen O'Connell, Rosemary Clooney, and at one time, Rosemarie), and a big comeback at Manhattan's Freddie's Supper Club which was so widely praised. In 1991, she, Connie Haines, former Tommy Dorsey band singer and Sinatra counterpart with that band, and Margaret Whiting climbed back on the Florida circuit with 3 Girls 3 and also went to Texas with the Mills Brothers all while recovering from foot surgery.

Kay is active in the wonderful organization so many of us support, the Los Angeles based Society of Singers, which helps singers get some tender, loving care, especially when in need, (I'm also a member without doing much but lending a little support). She also works to help her fellow Native Americans as a member of the board of the Los Angeles Indian Center.

At the release of the song *Wheel of Fortune*, the composer writes:
"While the Wheel is spinning, spinning, spinning,
I'll not dream of winning,
Fortune...or...fame."

Kay Starr never had long to dream about those goals, she won fortune and fame a long time ago, and she's still telling her stories to music.

Woody Herman
Relegated to the Cellar

"They said it was noise"

You'd think an intimate conversation with vintage, creative Jazz-artist, Woody Herman, would be held at a nostalgic reunion or memorial jazz concert or get-together. Not this time: the playlands of Eastern Long Island was the setting.

At 5 P.M. one early Summer evening in 1981, *Long Island PM Magazine* Editor Paul Raymond called me to say that he heard Herman was supposed to be performing a one-nighter out in the Hamptons where nightclub owner Stan Lerner had hired the band to perform at his posh, in-spot Le Mans disco. That's all I had to hear!

Photographer Camille Smith was not available on such short notice, so at 6:00 P.M., photographer, friend and part-time employee, Gus Young and I, with cold sandwiches and two cokes in a brown bag, drove out to Southampton in my old '69 Mercedes to the apex of Sunrise Highway and Hampton Road to see if we could find one Woody Herman. At that precise spot, we found what looked like a quonset-style, converted bowling alley. It was Le Mans all right, and it was barely an hour before opening time. There was Woody's Band Bus parked at the far end of the lot. We could not find Lerner anywhere on the premises, so our contact was gone with the wind and time was growing short. If we didn't talk to Woody now, we would have to wait until the show was over, and then, just maybe, they'd have no time for an interview and the trip would've been wasted.

We explored the club while the band tuned up. The entire place was auto-orientated. Tables were a tire above half an axle covered with glass, and seats were cut-off-parts of actual buses, cars, or anything that normally moved on the ground with wheels that had been

105

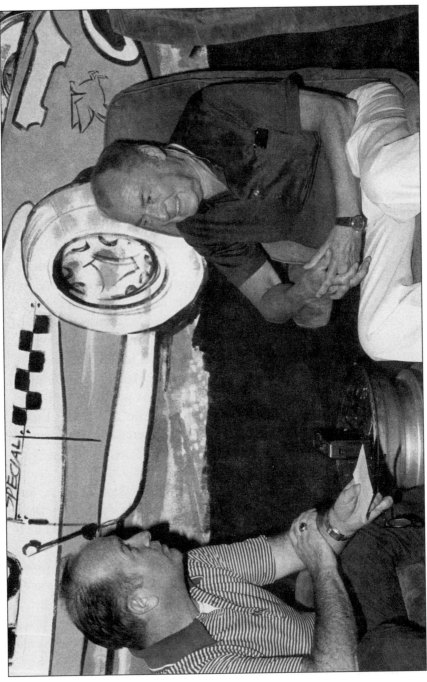

At Le Mans Club in Southampton with Woody before concert 1982. Photo by Gus Young.

converted to the nightclub's use. It was named after the famous race-track in LeMans, France.

With time running low, our search ended suddenly when we ran smack into Woodrow Charles Herman leaving the Men's Room where he must have been all along. We quickly corralled him. He was cordial and willing, but needed to get to rehearsal, so we hastily found a couple of seats in the nearby "Quiet Zone" and began our conversation with this very friendly midwesterner:

"It feels like I'm meeting a legend, and it feels good," I began as Gus Young set up his camera.

"That's because I've lasted longer that I should've. The only reason I'm a legend is because I am still alive and kicking," he said, chuckling, "I'm too old to retire and as long as I have reasonable health, I'll continue to work."

"I *love* the music but I *hate* the travel." responded my hero to the inevitable retirement question which I put away early. You sometimes detest those annoying inquiries you must put to these living icons, but how else can you get the answers you need.

Even though Woody spoke in that famous, pleasant drawl, and his age was beginning to show in his ever familiar face (he was 67 at the time), you knew he was unmistakably that lovable pint-sized giant whose "Band That Played The Blues" 1930's skyrocket ride is still legendary in and out of jazz circles. His renditions of *Caledonia* and *Apple Honey* alone would have been enough for me. But Woody will not dwell on the past even though he acknowledged it was important to his career. *Caledonia* and *Apple Honey* is simply history to Woody. His favorite record was unexpectedly "The one I'll make next year." He grinned and looked over to the bandstand which was now rehearsing in full swing.

"It's very boring to play the same old music. But, there are things that I'm proud of that were very good for the time. I'm interested to prove to anyone who cares to listen that I know where my roots are and that I am responsible for everything I've ever played. I never copped out and said the record producer made me do this or that. And I enjoy the music business or I couldn't do it for all these years. If everything remained the same and I had to play only the old things, I'd have thrown in the towel a long time ago."

And to my amazement, Woody disclosed his favorite instrument is not the clarinet, but rather the sax. "I feel I'm a better sax player, but when I was a young man it was important to play the American hot instrument of the day, and that was the clarinet."

At the age of just nine, Woody was already a vaudeville trouper, being billed as *The Boy Wonder of the Clarinet* when playing with local bands around Milwaukee, including Isham Jones. The boys first big hit was the *Woodchopper's Ball* in 1939, which is now an all-time jazz standard.

But, even after all this time, Woody is still riled up about booking agencies of yesterday and the record executives of today who run the music business: He recalled how he and Glenn Miller would sit in the outer offfices of booking agencies waiting to get to the inner offices: "They'd throw a dart at a map like they did 100 years ago and that's where you went. And it's still the same now. Today in Southampton and tomorrow in Columbus,...no kidding. The record industry today is also ran by accountants who have no knowledge of music and they don't want any," he revealed, "it's just a business with no feelings and they are evidently successful—so they must be right. They have relieved themselves of the responsibility of having creative people a long time ago."

It cost about $25,000.00 a week to keep the Herman band on the road. And that means 6 bookings out of 7 days. Payroll has to be met, plus the bus, hotel bills, commissions, and other expenses. That is an average amount for a band of this size. If the band had well-known sidemen, instead of young players, it would be even more. Add a vocalist and it gets bigger. Booking agencies say you break even the first four nights. If someone requests the band specifically, then the profit goes up, and maybe that's a seventh day, too.

For a moment or two we discussed comparisons of yesterday's and today's music; (1981) There's Billy Joel, Rush, Pink Floyd, and others, versus the Big Bands of the past: "Well there is a lot of material that has quality and there is a lot of garbage. But there was a lot of garbage 45 years ago. My music was not accepted by the mature person, *they said it was noise.* My records were bought by kids and their parents relegated them to the cellar with their phonograph." How poignant—I was one of them!

As of that day in 1981, Woody had been clearly out of the cellar for 44 years and was still part of the scene. The crowds continue to come—some are young and some are older. His sixteen players sitting on the bandstand a hundred feet away were very young, the average being 25.

"I consider myself a coach—a coach can be old, but not the players." he quipped, "You need energy to play." You couldn't help but notice Woody's slumped-forward shoulders and pale face. He seemed older than his years, like someone carrying great weight around, but you couldn't tell it by his enthusiasm. "Music constantly changes and that's one gratifying thing about the whole scene. It's completely different from the music of the forties."

Woody Herman is, of course, responsible for the success of many jazz greats including sax player Stan Getz and vibraphonist Terry Gibbs who were once band members. They still were getting together at annual reunions at Woody's home in the Hollywood Hills and at various festivals. In 1977, almost everyone from his past bands and herds showed up for his 40th anniversary performance at Carnegie Hall, "and they all played. Zoot Sims, The Candoli Brothers, Pete and Conte...Chubby Jackson, Don Lamond—they all came out. Then a few months ago we did the Monterey Jazz Festival and Getz was there and I had him do one of our charts."

Woody never arranged his charts, but he claims to be a very good editor. He kinda prides himself on his ability to make a young player give a better performance than he would ordinarily by rubbing off some of the *Herman* experience on him. That, I think, kept him musically sharpened and in tune with the continuous growth of music on a day-by-day basis, which explains his joy at staying in the business.

"Over 80 percent of my year is spent visiting high schools and colleges. What we do there," he went on, "is hold seminars with clinic sessions where our young men are utilized by players as teachers— so I learn from youth, being around them so much—it's a different environment so you are open to learning where most people my age are not."

Woody wouldn't let us go without telling us to tell you about his revered experience recording with Igor Stravinsky some years back. Stravinsky, then considered to be the world's greatest living composer, wrote a piece entitled *Ebony Concerto* just for his band. Woody called it the high point of his career with demure pride.

Woody admitted he has a lot of miles on him and reminded me that he has spent 44 years as a jazzman and the same amount of years married to the same woman.

"Which is a record for a jazz musician." he touted as we shook hands and exchanged goodbyes then watched him amble over to the bandstand, charts in hand, ready to play and lead his young players.

For a few years, before he died in 1986, Woody was harassed with overwhelming IRS claims which forced him to forfeit his home, which he bought from Humphrey Bogart and Lauren Bacall. His daughter, Ingrid Herman Reese, started a fund within the jazz community who rallied to help him out of his financial dilemmas. They said he owed the government 1.5 million, but they would never offer him a justifiable settlement.

The following year the Woody Herman "ghost band" hit the road. The phrase "ghost band" originated from Woody Herman's own lips, as if he knew.

Lionel Hampton spills the beans at Huntington's Harry Chapin Theater.

Volcano of Energy

Lionel Hampton

One of his early idols was jazz great Louis Armstrong: "Louis had come to L.A. without his regular backup band and so he asked us if we would back him in a recording session. Louis spotted a set of vibes (in the studio) and asked if I knew how to play them, which I did, since I knew the basic keyboard. (It was actually a vibraharp NBC used to use as its identification signal chime during station breaks.) That was the first known time jazz had been played on the vibes."

Lionel Hampton and Louis Armstrong recorded Eubie Blake's immortal *Memories of You* that day, and a young jazz buff named John Hammond heard it and rushed to L.A. to hear it live at the Paradise *Club* where Hamp was playing. The next evening, a hot August night in 1936, while Hamp was leading his band at the Paradise Club, a place where sailors bought a 25 cents pitcher of beer while they awaited their bus trip return to San Pedro and Long Beach bases in California, John Hammond and Benny Goodman dropped by and sparked a historic 3½ hour jam session before Benny and Lionel were ever introduced to each other, and it nearly tore off the roof. "I guess it was a little bit of nerve and a little luck thrown in for good measure." Lionel said.

"We were playing," he recalled, while we and WGSM radio's famous disk jockey Bruce Herbert conversed and rambled on with him for an hour before show time in a dressing room trailer behind the new, but incomplete, Harry Chapin Amphitheater in Huntington, Long Island's Hecksher Park. While munching on Burger-King Whoppers and Coca-Cola my son Jim had just brought in for us, he further reminisced, "then, the next thing I knew, there was Benny on stage during a break playing his clarinet. I looked over my shoulder and there was Gene Krupa banging away and Teddy Wilson smilin' at the piano. What a sound...it was unbelievable to me...I joined in with my vibes...and that was the *beginning* of the Benny Goodman Quartet." The very next day they recorded the legendary *Moonglow* and *Dinah*.

John Hammond had gotten them together. And, as they say, the rest is history: "Benny liked it so much he asked me to join his group. "It's amazing too, that Benny's ingenious coupling of Teddy Wilson and Lionel was inadvertently brave, even courageous, since black musicians simply didn't play in white bands in those days. But Benny was more concerned about the quality of the music than the racial problems that might be created. He didn't give a damn about the racial problems. "The people accepted us and did not seem to resent our playing together. But some of Benny's friends didn't like (or accept) it." Lionel said. They stuck together for four memorable years.

Lionel Hampton is the most outstanding vibraphonist of the Jazz Age, although he was originally a drummer. He is a volcano of energy who can carry thousands of people into a state of ecstasy by his sheer playing power and showmanship. He loves a big band behind him—trumpets, saxes, playing almost without consideration for intonation, blend, or any kind of precision. All of that simply adds to his own firepower.

Hamp humbly credits all his success to God, who he says "Gave me the talent," but it was his late wife, Gladys, who gave him the *inspiration* which still drives him today. She managed his business affairs and was his eyes, ears and the human power behind him. (He married her on Armistice Day in Yuma, Arizona, on his way to join Goodman in New York.)

It's an remarkable thing to see and feel the enthusiasm that Lionel Hampton generates at a performance. When I noticed him pause for a momentary prayer just before going on stage, I inquired about it:

"I always keep the faith—studied Bible through my grandmother—Mama Louvenia, I loved her so—she read me the psalms, so it's always in my mind. I give grace to the Lord every time I play on the bandstand."

Words from Lionel Hampton on WGSM Radio.

He once wrote a piece entitled *The King David Suite* while on a trip to Jerusalem, where he visited King David's tomb: "The music came to me in the tomb—I was inspired to write that work. I feel that God has a hand in everything we do. He puts all my ideas together and they always work."

Lionel always enjoys working live concerts and going from one city to another, unlike many other musicians who love the music but hate the monotonous traveling: "We always have a wonderful gathering everywhere we play and we meet old friends, just like you and Bruce here. It makes you tick. It gets you to meet with the people who admire your work. You got to let the people see you work—you got to do it—you're in the profession and you have to be out where you can test your skills to see if they are working or not, and if you are playing the right thing. The people react to it and then you know if you're on the right track."

Lionel's great wish is to have a distinguished band always and to have friends around him. "I would be loving-kind to them, and I want them to be loving-kind to me—and that's it!"

Hamp says he is 81 these days (1995), but some say he's defying the historians and it's calculated that he's really a few years older (actually 87 being born in 1908.). Over the years he has formed a kid's scholarship fund he calls the Lionel Hampton Development Center which is dear to his heart. You can always find him at work on it raising funds at every opportunity. While we spoke I verified the legendary story of how he discovered two great jazz singers in a single day.: "A little girl named Ruth Jones who worked in the powder room of a club (Garrett's Bar in Chicago), where I was playing, and sometimes worked for Walter Fuller's Quintet, came out and sang for me and I hired her on the spot. I instantly changed her name to *Dinah Washington*, but she didn't care what I called her so long as I gave her a job with my band. Another fellow auditioned on the same day later on after the matinee, and I hired him on the spot, too. His name was *Joe Williams*." Joe was a doorman at the Regal Theater, and wound up staying with Hamp for a year or so and Dinah for about the same they moved on. It was Lionel who introduced the perennial and extraordinary Quincy Jones to the world of music. It was, also, with a Hampton band that Nat King Cole first achieved fame as a vocalist.

And you can add the names of Betty Carter and Aretha Franklin as Hampton discoveries, too.

Further Hampton band graduates include Clark Terry, Fats Navarro, Charlie Mingus, Wes Montgomery, Art Farmer, Dexter Gordon, and Illinois Jacquet. Hamp is a man of tremendous zest, who lives and breathes music, whose vitality is contagious, and who loves his fellow beings. No complaints. Just enthusiasm and accommodation. He seems comfortable with tributes and celebrations of his music and his celebrity status. In 1983 he was honored at the Kennedy Center in Washington and at the White House, where he's been many times before. A friend and supporter of President Reagan, a Special Events Director for President Ford, he was also the first black to lead his orchestra at a Presidential Inaugural Ball—Harry Truman's back in 1949—and has played for seven Presidential Inaugurations since. He's been an Ambassador of Music to the United Nations, a Human Rights Commissioner in New York City and honored at a Lionel Hampton Day under the Arch de Truimphe in Paris, France. He possesses numerous Doctorates at many Universities across the U.S. and has established the Lionel Hampton Jazz Endowment Fund across U.S. campuses.

"My music has certainly taken me a long way from Holy Rosary Academy back in Kenosha, Wisconsin," he reminisced. "I learned from strict Catholic Dominican Sisters, you know. That's why I'm so disciplined. That's why I work so hard."

Well, since he recorded his classic theme song, *Flying Home* in 1942, shortly after he left Goodman to form his own group, the band always includes a version of that recording in every concert, usually at the opening. (The original recording included sidemen Dexter Gordon and Illinois Jacquet.) That night, while out front, I actually heard someone say in a whisper, as if Lionel could actually hear him over the band's great vibration, "Play like Hell, Lionel, Play like Hell." Young and old alike were dealt a wildly swinging version of his celebrated evergreen. They cried aloud: "More, More," and the crescendos grew louder and louder and the band was swinging almost wildly.

Today, besides playing like a crazy 25 year old, Hamp endows scholarships and lectures against drugs, when he plays at high schools. He fulfills his annual obligation to teach and perform at the

Lionel Hampton School of Music at the University of Idaho. He tours and tours tirelessly. He keeps his band full of men young, and acts and plays accordingly. "I play with young cats...I got lots of good guys."

You have to know him to fully understand it all. When he's home in his high-rise overlooking Lincoln Center, you can find him quietly playing Thelonious Monks' *Round Midnight* on the vibes sometimes at three in the morning. Then he looks up and declares to any visitor or friend: "We got a helluva band. The best in the Country."

It's still true, and it's 1995. It's truly astounding. Eighty-six and performing live at the Blue Note he records a session, sells 25,000 recordings in the first two weeks of release and winds up with a Grammy nomination, then promptly signs a contract with Mojazz, the new jazz division of Motown.

He is currently accepting international bookings through 1996. Anything else you want to know?

Talking backstage with the Divine Sarah.

The Original Divine One

'Sassy Sings'

I first heard Sarah Lois Vaughan sing in the flesh while conversing backstage with Tony Bennett at Westbury Music Fair: "Isn't it wonderful to do an interview with Sarah singing in the background. I feel so inspired when I listen to her!" he said. While I talked to Tony, it was clear that Sarah was very much with us spiritually, while actually only a few hundred feet away live on stage singing to a packed house.

About an hour later Sarah Vaughan and I sat face-to-face on a soft leather couch in her dressing room between shows. Sarah, dressed in a very casual dressing gown, had one eye on the conclusion of a television soap opera and one eye on me fiddling with a recorder, getting ready to put her words on tape.

We talked awhile about her early association with that band of jazz innovators, Dizzy Gillespie, Budd Johnson, Charlie Parker and Billy Eckstine, when they played together in the famous Earl (Fatha) Hines Band. After all, it was Billy who discovered Sarah while he was singing with Earl, and he induced Earl to hire her. Dizzy and Sarah worked up some great duets with Sarah on piano (—Yes, piano! She was taught piano and organ from the age of seven years.) Most, unfortunately were never recorded because the recording ban was in effect at that time due to striking musicians. There is however, one existing recording of Dizzy and Sarah with her on the piano.

Nevertheless, Sarah states much of her musical development occurred during that alliance. Billy formed his own band in 1944, leaving the Earl to play more conservative material, taking along Sarah, Budd, and Dizzy. It was the beginning of the new and exciting sounds of BeBop. (Billy also hired a budding star by the name of Miles Davis who was also just starting out.) The band was on a be-

121

bop kick and blossomed with the help of this generally timid young performer from Newark, New Jersey (She was 20.) who sang with so much innovation and feeling...

"I listen to the musicians, the horn players, more than anything. That's where I get my stuff. I steal a lot. I'm a big thief. I just do it different so I don't get caught. My hands are my heart." Some have tried to cast jazz singer Sarah as a blues singer, which she is not. Sarah once told music writer Gene Lees, "...I am *not* and never have been a blues singer," But, Gene adds in his book *Singers and the Song,* "she is also a gospel singer. There is a great deal of church in her work." I agree with Lees when he contends that Sarah brings emotion to the surface by coloring the sounds in her almost supernaturally controlled throat, not in the usual way of imitating speech patterns in the reading of a lyric.

However, I cannot help but compare young Mariah Carey to early Sarah. Mariah too has the qualities apparent in the very young Sarah. Mariah's belief in what she delivers musically, punctuating each word and accentuating feelings, stressing important phrases with body and hand action, is similar to Sarah's use of arms and hands that accentuate the song's story. For instance, there's her timeless renditions of *Don't Blame Me* (my favorite), *Body & Soul, I Should Care,* and *I Cried For You.* (Sarah's first break came with her performance of *Body & Soul* sung at an amateur contest in Harlem's famed Apollo Theater where Billy Eckstine first heard her.) In other more socially tolerant times Sarah might have been a candidate for grand opera. She had the complete command of the harmonic materials of songs.

Over her career, Sarah Vaughan, who won the Downbeat polls of 1973 and 1975, has sung in over 60 countries in every place from intimate night clubs to stadiums with over 100,000 in attendance. She has performed with the Boston Pops, the San Francisco Symphony, and the Los Angeles Philharmonic. She has recorded endless singles and albums, although for a five year period in the late sixties, she had no recording contract but continued to tour internationally.

Somewhat direct when asked, Sarah admires her peers: "If the material is good, if the melody is good, and if the person singing it catches my ear, then it's good music that I can like. If an artist knocks me out—I listen. I can't stand screaming voices when you can't hear the lyrics."

You feel very good in the presence of Sarah—you really do. She is smooth and yet demure. Her genuine sincerity shines through the warmth of each expression and the marvelously clear, vibrant voice. Sarah's voice is actually three voices: soprano, alto, and baritone and she mixes them excellently when and where she needs to and has such consummate control of vibrato, especially true in her later years.

Everyone calls Sarah by a different nickname. William B. Williams of New York's WNEW simply called her *Sass*: Billy Eckstine extends it to *Sassy*. Her sobriquet is really *The Divine One.* Her business card says" "The Divine One." Some call her *Divine Sarah,* and still others, *The Great Sarah.*

Sarah was just under twenty-five when she began her some 60 odd recordings for Columbia and was associated with some of the best arrangers and sidemen in the business. With a naive voice and great musicianship, she scored heavily with this group of recordings which established her forever as a great artist. The sessions with Columbia lasted four short years and all her later recordings would reflect a much deeper and lower tone, like the one we heard today.

I was really in awe of Sarah Vaughan while in her presence and I don't know exactly why. Maybe it was her pristine past and great reputation. Maybe her legendary status among all the great popular singers. I guess in my mind I placed her on a pedestal like a handful of others who have profoundly penetrated my life with their gifts of music that have become so familiar and comfortable, and maybe I feel that I owe her and those others so much that I could never repay them, if I lived another hundred years.

After Sarah Vaughan passed on from cancer in 1990 at the age of 66, there was a tribute at Carnegie Hall. Bill Cosby emceed and Dizzy played and Roberta Flack sang Sarah's own *Tenderly.* There was much emotion backstage, but what really gave the night its release of grief were the comments of Billy Eckstine. "She was my little sister, my baby," Billy said with a catch in his voice, "...and I loved her very much."

Perry Sings Round & Round.

Perry Como

The Barber From Canonsburg

Perry Como and I go way back to the days of good old radio. He was working his durable pipes on a fifteen-minute NBC show three nights a week in studio 6-A, Rockefeller Center. I was a studio page wearing one of those classy blue uniforms with a yellow braid over one shoulder and a monogrammed lapel pin the shape of a microphone on the other. Perry and I would always exchange a few words before the show about, of course, the show, and how many people might show up for the performance. That studio was also the weekly home of The Bell Telephone Hour, a weekly one hour program of classical and semi-classical music where outstanding vocalists like Ezio Pinza and Marion Anderson performed.

Perry always acquired inspiration from the imposing abilities of those greats. And we often talked about that, too. His popular program was called the *Chesterfield Supper Club*. It later made a successful transition to television, unlike many other radio shows, also for 15 minutes and similarly sponsored by the cigarette company.

In those days, Perry was crooning his tremendous hits *Till the End of Time, A Hubba-Hubba-Hubba, Because, Some Enchanted Evening, When You Were Sweet Sixteen,* and *Temptation.* He had come a long way from those barber shop days in the small coal-mining town of Canonsburg, Pa. where, on May 18, 1912, he was born to Italian immigrant parents of 12 other children. At the age of 14 he actually owned his own barber shop where customers always got their money's worth. Besides shaving and grooming them, he entertained customers by singing popular tunes. Then, in 1933, one of the musicians who was also Perry's customer and a member of the popular Freddie Carlone Band, carried an offer to him from Carlone for 28 dollars a week

Perry Como and mentor Bing Crosby.

singing and traveling with the band. Perry happily accepted and was on his way.

"I remember when Perry sang (later) for Ted Weems." Frankie Laine said to me when we were talking about his own career, "Perry was always a kind guy and got me a tryout with Freddy Carlone, just when I needed employment the most, but I didn't last but a few weeks...my music and his music clashed." Perry and Frank have remained lifelong friends.

Perry traveled with the Weems Band during the following years, perfecting his mellow vocal style. During the war years the band had a hard time keeping together, so Perry returned to Pennsylvania and resumed barbering. Encouraged by his childhood sweetheart, Roselle Belline, now his wife for over 60 years, Perry answered an offer from CBS to star in his own radio show. He returned to the music business, signed his first recording contract with RCA and released his first record, *Long Ago and Far Away*. He remained with RCA for over 40 years, their longest running association with any performer, after all, he amassed an enviable list of hits, 42 of them in the Top 10 between 1944 and 1958, second only to Bing Crosby.

It was *Don't Let the Stars Get in Your Eyes, A Bushel and A Peck, Papa Loves Mombo, Catch A Falling Star,* and *Wanted* during the fifties.

Perry tried the movies but the big screen did not adequately project his personality, so he turned to television in 1955 and became the stunning star of a very high quality, hour-long variety show that lasted 8 years. At the end of each show, Perry would sit in a cardigan perched on a stool next to a music stand and a red rose and just sing. His relaxed informality became a part of nearly every listening household. Songs like *Hot Diggity, Round and Round, Magic Moments,* and *Delaware* were spun by musical director Mitchell Ayres and offered by Perry from the heart with the help of the girl singing group, The Fontane Sisters. One segment of the show featured requests: The girls would sing, "Letters, we get letters, we get stacks and stacks of letters. Dear Perry, would you be so kind; to fill a request and sing the song I like best?" And, of course, Perry would answer the request for a thrilled listener.

Then came rock and roll and things changed. Perry reminded us that in 1970 it was Richard Rodgers who said: "This is the era of mediocrity. The kids can't play their instruments, they don't know anything about music, they buy a $3 dollar guitar and go in the bathroom and make a record and it sells nine million."

"It's crazy, but it's true," said Perry. "For years, singers like Vic Damone, Steve Lawrence, and many others were unable to get recording contracts. Now, people like Tony Bennett are reinventing our kind of music, and thank God for radio and 'Music of Your Life' stations all over the country who still play our stuff."

In June of 1970, for the first time in 25 years, Perry Como appeared "live," and it was at The International Hotel in Las Vegas. Later that year, *It's Impossible became his twentieth gold disc. The songs, Seattle* and *And I Love You* were also great '70's hits for Perry. At the age of sixty (he always looked like he was 35) he began a world tour. His *40 Greatest Hits* was a million-seller in the United Kingdom, and did very well in Japan and Italy, too. His annual TV Christmas Show became an American institution.

In 1982, Perry played sell-out concerts in Manila and Japan, and starred in a TV special from Paris for ABC, with Angie Dickinson as his guest.

I remember once at a Westbury Music Fair concert in 1986, a vendor in the lobby theater kept hawking, "Seventy-Two years old, fifty years in the business. Buy a book here," trying to sell Como souvenir magazines. He led off that concert with, *The Best of Times*, that set the tone for the evening.

Mickey Glass has been Perry Como's manager and overall business guardian for over 50 years and still runs Perry's career from an office on Northern Boulevard in Great Neck, Long Island, with the help of Vera Hamilton, longtime secretary. "Perry doesn't like hectic things, but he likes the audience. They're his friends out there," Vera said, "and Perry is a genuinely nice guy."

When I wrote to Perry Como in 1992, enclosing a copy of an article featuring Bing Crosby and those singers who followed him that I had just completed for a California magazine, Perry replied saying, "Bing was one of my idols in those early years. I used to imitate the

Bing and Russ Columbo styles which were the most popular of that time of my career."

Perry says he misses those days in New York and the many friends he made there over the years. Although he spent most of his life in Sands Point, Long Island, he now lives in his long-time West Palm Beach, Florida, vacation home, where he regularly plays golf. "The only hair I cut now is for my grandchildren...but, they're terrible tippers," he grins.

I always enjoyed the tribute that New York Times music critic, John S. Wilson conferred upon both Perry Como and Bing Crosby:

"The qualities that go into the making of a great pop singer are so changeable, so subject to the whims of fashion, that it is difficult to pin them down. Even within the context of a given period and a given style, the great pop singers are a complex mixture of voice, personality, sensitivity and taste—to mention just a few of the ingredients. Some singers find the key early and maintain it throughout their careers, as Bing Crosby did and Perry Como does..."

**Fran Warren through the looking glass at Northstage Theater,
Glen Cove, NY, 1983.**

Fran Warren

Something Special from the Bronx

Hurrah for gutsy Fran Warren, the hip Bronxite kid who grew up a few subway stops from the 1940's hot Harlem jazz spots, who was initially inspired by the legendary Billie Holiday and urged on by earliest musical friend and sponsor, Billy Eckstine and wound up girl singer in the sensational Charlie Barnet band, when she was just this side of eighteen. Her illustrious career has moved ahead enthusiastically ever since right up 'til the present. She played out a lengthy 1994 Hawaiian gig, and without taking a breath, got herself set for a Northeast club tour which included Boston, Philadelphia and even New Jersey. Her benefit work throughout 1995 with the Society of Singers in L.A. just adds to the long list.

My first encounter with Fran Warren was in old Glen Cove, on Long Island's Gold Coast, where she appeared for the first time as "Mame" at the Northstage dinner-theater, a then newly-renovated proscenium stage which was converted from a 1927 vaudeville house. There she laid them in the aisles with her heartwarming rendition of *If He Walked Into My Life Today*.

You, no doubt, will remember Fran as the magical teen-age vocalist for Claude Thornhill when she recorded one of the big band era's most enduring classics, *Sunday Kind of Love*. It's still the song that most identifies her.

"I received only fifty dollars to record that song, but I built my whole career around it." she acknowledged. When she performs that charming evergreen at places like Michael's Pub in Manhattan, it always brings down the house and dampens a few cheeks, and like Kay Starr says, "Someone reaches out and touches somebody and you can just feel the memories starting."

This girl has done everything and more. She has performed in *Pajama Game,* played Adelaide in *Guys And Dolls,* Nellie Forbush in

131

South Pacific, Sharon in *Finian's Rainbow,* Lorelei in *Gentleman Prefer Blondes,* Dolly in *Once More With Feeling,* Linda in *Flower Drum Song,* and even in a revival of *The Big Broadcast* with Harry James. She is always a sell out at jazz club engagements in Manhattan. Overall, Fran has recorded 700 singles, over 20 albums, in almost 50 years of singing. And she looks half her age.

Back in 1943 she was known in the neighborhood by her given name, Fay Wolfe. A sixteen year old hopeful, one day she ventured out quite alone and scared to legendary 52nd Street, then the Mecca of jazz, to see and hear a singer named Frances Fay and a chance meeting with young singer, Billy Eckstine, who invited her to a club across the street to hear Billie Holiday. Billie learned she was an aspiring singer and invited her to sing by personally leading her to the bandstand, saying, "Sing it pretty." The song was Gershwin's *Embraceable You* and Fran sang her heart out. Remaining until 2 A.M., it was Billy Eckstine who took her home to worried parents who had expected her back much earlier. Some months later it was a concerned Billy Eckstine who telephoned her to tell her to use the nom-de-plume *Fran Warren* for her career name.

"Where did you get such a name?" she asked, "Well, there's a bootleg wine called 'Warren's Sweet Wine', it's a good name, kid, and it looks good on you, so don't argue with me—use it!" And she did. "It just worked better than Fay Wolfe," Billy told me many years later.

When she was able to audition for girl singer in Duke Ellington's famous orchestra, the Duke dutifully took her aside and told her, "Listen, honey. You can't sing with this band."

Frantic, Fran asked, "Don't I sing good enough?" and the Duke replied empathetically, "Yes, you do. But, listen to me. When you become eighteen and when Charlie Barnet's Band comes to New York—you go see him and tell him *I* sent you to him. That's the band you should be singing with."

Fran Warren was too young to read the racial message that she eventually had to experience for herself. Being brought up in a black and white environment, her parents had to explain the difference between white and black as it applied in the outside world.

"It's just not accepted that Mr. Ellington could hire you no matter how good you were. It would not work." Her father's words rung out to her but she viewed them at the time as pure insanity.

"But I took his advice, and auditioned for Barnet—and Kay (Starr) was just leaving—so he hired me. We opened at the Apollo a few days later and it was wonderful. It was the real beginning for me and I knew I was in the business to stay. "

Now, over 45 years later, she is still essentially a vocalist whose reviews are always sprinkled with mentions of those peerless qualities and strong emotional depth she invariably lends to a singing performance. She is the prototypical girl band singer who easily made the transition to musical comedy.

"I am a singer who acts—rather than an actress who sings. It's a complete turn-around for the theater. When I do night club work, I do over twenty songs in a few hours. That's *really* work. I can talk to you in the small night club audience—that's something you can't do in the theater. But, I love them both."

Her "Happy Pad" is a West Side Manhattan apartment in a suite that was once occupied by composer Johnny Burke (of Burke and Van Heusen), which she had previously occupied many years before when she first left the Bronx to go out on her own. When she returned much later to Manhattan, after living in California a number of years, her manager coincidentally found the very same apartment for her. She was ecstatic and happy to be close to friends and the clubs and places where she performed.

Backstage in Glen Cove, Fran Warren and I talked about the many sides of her life, including the down side—the crisis that nearly destroyed her career. It first started in 1964 with headlines like "Bag Singer, Kin Over Dope" and ended in 1978 when she won a $400,000 settlement from the city for that same false arrest. The experience made her political, but she feels government can quell the drug situation. "Drugs are here because somebody is paying off the law—the corruption is unbelievable."

Later, Fran was to face other family difficulties involving her family with respect to alleged "bogus" stress and diet clinics her husband and daughter operated. The U.S. Attorney's office prosecuted them as backers of the clinics which they contended were operating illegitimately. They faced prison as a result of this trial. All this took its toll on Fran Warren, but she did not allow her vocal talents to go fallow.

So there we were in a little town, in a little theater, in a little dressing-room, talking heavy stuff. It was about the collection of scattered voices and players who make up the Big Band Era, but who mostly pass each other like ships in the night, the latter observed by both Woody Herman and Harry James.

Fran Warren possesses a conspicuous bravura quality, so evident in her performances, especially when she sings such songs as *Over the Rainbow* and *Hello Young Lovers*. Tonight it is *Mame*. Very soon a recording date. After that a European Tour. Hawaii? Russia? A television show? And on, and on.

Fran Warren is a wonderful experience. *Wonderful* is the only word.

One of the Great Four

Teddy Wilson, With Benny, Gene, & Lionel
August 1981

When I think of the great piano players of the Big Band Era, Teddy Wilson always prevails in my mind as the most accomplished, the most easy to listen to and the most mysterious. Some of the best music ever made has to be those outstanding sides Billie Holiday recorded with Teddy Wilson's very fine orchestra during 1939, the one and only year he led his own band. "Our band only lasted a year or so. We were too tame. Everybody then expected a black band to be more exiting. We made some great recordings. We had Ben Webster, Doc Cheatham, J.C. Heard and played a lot at the Famous Door nightclub on 52nd Street," said Teddy.

Teddy Wilson learned to play the piano while in grade school and developed his style with a dance band in high school, where he, also, played oboe and clarinet. He went on to classical musical training for a year at Taladega College in Alabama. He was a disciplined student mostly owing to the fact that both his parents were teachers at Samuel Houston College, when he was a child. Talladega spawned his life-long love of classical music, but jazz remained his first love and in the summer of 1929 he migrated to Detroit where he began his career with the Speed Webb band. He then moved on to Toledo and Chicago with the Milton Senior Band.

It was John Hammond, the most enthusiastic and influential jazz buff around in those days, who discovered Teddy: "He helped me a great deal—perhaps more than anyone, except the players them-selves." Teddy and I were talking about old times and old music at MacArthur Airport in Ronkonkoma, Long Island, where he was preparing to perform for the local Arts Council summer evening jazz concert. We were sitting in his Cadillac—me in the back and he and

At a windy arrival MacArthur Airport, Ronkonkoma, L.I. in 1981.
Photo by Gus Young.

his secretary up front—articulating his life and times. The interview was held in the car because it was so windy near the airfield that words were inaudible and you had to shout to be heard.

Teddy was really a shy celebrity, almost unwilling to talk too much or expand on topics affecting his life, and peculiarly unwilling to talk about his old friend and fellow musician, Benny Goodman. I didn't know why, but Budd Johnson later told me that Teddy felt that everyone was more interested in Benny Goodman, when they spoke to him, so he simply refused to honor any questions that included Benny Goodman in order not to be totally eclipsed by his former leader. It's a bit ironic because Benny Goodman once called Teddy Wilson, "the greatest musician irrespective of instrument." Actually, Teddy only played with Goodman for three years, but is most remembered for that time and exposure, although they later had a few reunions including one at the Brussels World Fair in 1958 and the famous Goodman Russian tour in 1962. And then there was the Benny Goodman Story movie where Teddy portrayed himself.

When I reminded him of his influence on piano players who followed him, like Art Tatum, The McPartlands, Mel Powell, and Joe Bushkin, his reply was simple: "Well, I am pleased and flattered, but they are really their own people. After all, I played in the tradition of Earl Hines, Fats Waller and Fletcher Henderson. They helped me, you know!" His typically humble rationale.

"Every day playing is my favorite day. I loved playing with the old quartet (Goodman quartet with Lionel Hampton and Gene Krupa). I enjoyed playing with Mel Torme at Carnegie Hall in 1980. (Mel and Friends—A George Wein weekend with George Shearing, Gerry Mulligan, Woody Herman and others.)

Teddy also taught at Juilliard and the Metropolitan Music Schools in Manhattan in the forties and fifties. I particularly remembered a Saturday afternoon weekly radio program on CBS when I was a kid when he played beautifully for half-an-hour. It consisted mostly of a delicately swinging piano and some delightful non-flashy classics. I always wondered if anyone kept the transcriptions. They would make a great album.

Teddy never expected to become a world-class musician when he started out: "I always wanted to play and I arrange all my own music.

I was lucky as I got a good start with Benny in Chicago on a radio show for Elgin watches." That was the only time he mentioned Benny Goodman during our half-hour interview.

"I like my life better now. I do better in small groups. I could be featured better that way. It is less on the nerves with more time for practicing... than running a big band."

I wondered, as I wonder about all those musicians who, as Woody Herman said, have lots of miles on them, why they travel so much at that time of their life:

"It's the money. The one night stands pay well. It's hard to say no, and the folks get a chance to see and hear you."

At this time of his life, Teddy does mostly freelance work alone and in a trio composed of him and his two sons. "I do a lot of what we're doing tonight...like an all-star group."

When I asked him how he would want people to remember him, his reply was: "You don't think about things like that. I'm headed overseas right after this and we'll be back in September. I feel great. I'm gonna' live forever."

It turns out Teddy Wilson had cancer at the time of the interview, and the hospital visit a few weeks before in upstate Syracuse, New York was for treatment, but he didn't want his condition known. He continued to tour throughout the world either as a soloist or with his trio, his career ending only a few months before his death in New Britain, Connecticut on July 31, 1986. He was 73. Teddy Wilson proved that jazz could be both elegant and exciting, and entertained us for the greater part of this century. I was honored by my short friendship of this self-effacing giant of jazz.

On the bandstand with Larry Elgart.

Larry Elgart

Hooked on the Ambassador of Swing

London, Connecticut born Larry Elgart is one of the recent giants of swing. Strongly influenced by the playing of Benny Goodman on his boyhood crystal radio set, his early contributions consisted of stints playing both alto and soprano sax in the popular bands of Tommy Dorsey, Charlie Spivak, and Woody Herman at the age of six-teen. During the 1950's, Larry and his older brother Les managed a very popular touring band begun in 1947. Their first Columbia recording entitled *Sophisticated Swing* made them an overnight sensa-tion. Larry was the genius, the mixer, the editor, and the acknowl-edged manager; in fact, he was the colorful, enthusiastic saxist, next to his brother who was rather lethargic. Larry imbued the band with so much spirit that eventually most of the other players began looking to Larry as the real leader.

The Elgart Touch, his well-known and graceful, stylistic phrasing musical stamp, with heavy emphasis on reeds and brass performed with minimal electronic amplification, clearly identifies him. It was the result of exceptionally fine arrangements by Bill Finegan (later partner in the Sauter-Finegan Organization), Charlie Albertine, and the genius of Nelson Riddle, who later was to help catapult Frank Sinatra's career into a stunning comeback success just when Sinatra needed it most.

Larry's classic solo rendition of *Harlem Nocturne* is creamy and full of dynamic nuances and truly a joy to listen to. To some it con-jures up navy blue midnights and desolate New York streets in the morning's wee hours. It's a mood song and seems to inspire the ladies in his audiences.

In 1953 it was he and Charlie Albertine who composed the televi-sion *American Bandstand* theme, *Bandstand Boogie,* when it was being aired on a local Philadelphia television station with a young man at the helm by the name of Dick Clark. And you should hear his swinging version of Joe Garland's *In The Mood.*

Larry and I exchanged some quality big band talk together at radio station WLIM's first birthday party in the mid-eighties and also at his New York City apartment on East 74th Street, when he was riding the crest with his tremendously successful *Hooked on Swing* album (47 weeks on the charts along with Michael Jackson and the Rolling Stones, and two-million sold—his 51st album). "I have a new career now," he said, "touring in concert to many college campuses in the U.S. It's a great thrill to see so many young people in the audience. They often come backstage to tell me how much they like this *new music—swing.*" he laughed. Then he told me about a man from California who wrote him and said the *Hooked* album brought him back into the record shops—the first time in 15 years—the last time he bought his wife a record album.

Although his latest band, first known as the Manhattan Swing Orchestra, and later renamed the Hooked on Swing Orchestra, achieved immense success with the new album and three successive albums, Larry was never to become as well-known as Goodman, Miller, Ellington, or Basie. That was mostly because he came on the scene somewhat later when indifferent Top Forty radio stations, who dominated radio time with only rock and roll, eclipsed exposure of most big band music on the airwaves.

Hooked on Swing was Larry's concept of the composite themes and old medleys of many of the Big Bands. The album placed his name back on the marqueés, despite the heavy emphasis on rock and roll. The music of Larry Elgart got through the maze and out in front of the record-buying public. *Hooked on Swing* became the best-selling swing music album ever.

And when *Hooked on Swing II* came out, radio station WLIM's Jack Ellsworth couldn't believe it: "It's a miracle. It's even better than the first one." It was true, being the best Big Band and most original swing album released in years. Lynn Elgart told me the album required four months of research for the six categories (picked among dozens) and the work was incredible.

Lynn, Larry's lovely wife, is clearly his best promoter and greatest fan, always keeping in touch with me when it came to Larry's accomplishments and performances itinerary. "The final press will be 300,000 copies." she bubbled, "the album is perfect, no cuts, no 'clams', and no editing required. All perfect takes. The arrangements on the album were done by Dick Hyman, Sy Johnson, Mike Abene, Dick Lieb, and Jack Cortner—masters all. Larry's musicians play with fresh vitality that is inspiring," she said, "theirs are fresh, new arrangements of familiar tunes. The material is alive."

Larry is a playing leader. He turns his players on by enthusiastically playing while leading. An electronic engineer, he mixes and edits, and acts as producer. He is involved in the total product. "Swing is a feeling," he says, "this is a dream band playing."

As he explained to me one day out at WLIM: "I've always been hooked on swing. It is a valid musical form that will live on forever, always taking new shape. It's the kind of music that people react to in an active, positive way. It is always listenable and always danceable, and most importantly, it's a happy form of music. We are not into nostalgia. By fusing contemporary rhythm with the pulse of swing, we have made the music of the Swing Era something today's youth can relate to. The music was fun then...and should be fun now."

Today, Larry Elgart is still a very vital human being living a comfortable existence in the Florida Keys with Lynn, running 5 miles a day on the beach and playing golf. In 1992 he traveled to Australia for the second time where he premiered his 53rd album, *Latin Obsession* at the Sydney Opera House and the Victoria Arts Centre in Melbourne. He will always be strong for his music and for life.

We have the King of Swing, the Count of Swing, the Duke of Swing, and now, approaching 74, Larry Elgart's impeccable musical taste, his use of imaginative arrangements, and his unique ability to translate swing music into the sound of the nineties, have earned him the admirable title, Ambassador of Swing. Well deserved, don't you think?

Listening to jazzmaster Budd Johnson at Burt Bacharach's in East Norwich, L.I. Photo by Gus Young.

Budd Johnson

A Life of Jazz
The Musician's Musician

In 1982, in the rural Long Island hamlet of East Norwich, the prolific songwriter Burt Bacharach owned an old wayside restaurant known as the East Norwich Inn. Alongside it, he built a modern, quality New York Hotel style inn where my wife and I spent many great get-a-way weekends relaxing and enjoying its ambiance and good food, and plotting out new fiction. My friend Bob Hope, also, used to reside there during his annual appearances at nearby Westbury Music Fair.

This very old Inn was the setting for one of the most inspiring interviews I have ever conducted. The subject was Budd Johnson, one of the most exciting and original musicians of Big Band Era's jazz age. A catalytic figure in the modern jazz movement, the inspirational legacy of this man, the sterling saxophonist who passed on from us in October of 1985 at the age of 73, transcended jazz styles. As a player and arranger, his ability to create can be heard on the recordings of many bands for whom he worked so hard, including those of Earl Hines, Count Basie and Dizzy Gillespie, (he worked in the first bebop recording session with Dizzy and Coleman Hawkins) and in the output of many small groups he either led or simply inspired. On each performance, then and now, Budd drives with the kind of old-fashioned strength and imagination of tenor playing that he helped establish while a bandsman with Earl Hines and Billy Eckstine in the early days, even though he is in his seventies. "I mostly played the reeds—all of them. But I best like arranging now."

Billy specifically told me that: "I think the success of my band was mainly due to the arrangements of Budd." Billy gave up his band because it was too much work and too expensive to operate. (He wearied of the racism, too. The entire band had to use the rear door, even where they performed.)

Budd was the quintessential team player. He was really a leader, but you'd never know it. He arranged much of what he played, but you'd never know that either.

We sat and talked for hours over a very unpretentious lunch. It was the answer to the question I've heard so many times: "Who is this Budd Johnson?" And when he talked about his grandson, his warmth and humanity shown through even brighter. I learned so much about him of which so little is written. His affection for the music and feelings for his fellow players surpassed his need to talk about himself.

Reaching back, Budd talked about how early jazz musicians consistently strived to improve their playing. He claimed, unlike many printed stories to the contrary by various critics, the early bands *were* well disciplined despite lack of formal training of some musicians and lack of money to buy the best instruments available. "The dedication to the early jazz movement was not planned—" he explained. "It just developed." Most bands had a good nucleus—the majority of the players having been together for many years so they sound as *one*. "Everybody's breathing alike and thinking alike." he declared, "it's a musical coup to get all the right guys together. That," he explained further, "is why I try to choose players whom I feel share a stylistic kinship and expression." Then he would arrange accordingly to highlight their individuality.

Once, Neal Hefti left the Basie organization and traveled to California to work for the movies. When he returned to New York, Budd met him in Birdland one night and Hefti complained: "Damn—I can't for the life of me get the sound out of the same arrangements I did with Basie—in my own band—we just don't sound right..." Budd reminded him that after playing twenty-five years together Basie's men all know each move everybody's gonna make.... "so it comes out better."

He told me the little known tale about the time Ben Webster came up to his hotel room while they were on tour and asked him to teach him saxophone. Ben was a piano player for the band. Budd went to work on Ben teaching him scales first and had Ben work on a song

Singing the Blues, which was a favorite of Webster's. In about eight months Ben began playing *saxophone* instead of piano. The rest is history, Ben Webster became one of the great tenor saxophonists.

Budd Johnson's best work of record is the fine material he accomplished while with the Basie Band, but he is really best-known for his key role as saxophonist-arranger with the Earl Hines Band of the thirties. But you have to step even a little further back to when he began being taught piano and basic music by the daughter of Booker T. Washington. This was soon after his first music lessons taught to him by his father, who played the organ and cornet. Along the way he developed an interest in playing the tenor sax, much like Webster, subsequently serving with many early bands up through the thirties including stints with Louis Armstrong and Fletcher Henderson. He has played and arranged for Woody Herman, Don Redman, and Buddy Rich, and was the musical director for Billy Eckstine's Orchestra. He has played with Sy Oliver, Cab Calloway, Benny Goodman, and the Tommy Dorsey Bands. He has toured the world with many groups and bands along the way.

"I haven't reached the highlight of my career, though," he said thoughtfully, believingly, "I want to sit down—take the time it needs—to write a serious piece. I want to complete a jazz symphony and try to sell it to a record company. You can beat the pavement to death trying to find a recording company to give you a date!"

Budd Johnson has played and arranged for so many bands, you couldn't possibly mention them all. But, again, you'd never know it. He was a kind of cornerstone along with a handful of others who quietly helped develop all that jazz everyone only talks about.

After spending an afternoon with him you realize he had such a clear understanding of his abilities he never had to show his ego. He was never a public figure, he was strictly a musician's musician.

**Johnny Mince circa 1939 with the Glenn Miller Orchestra.
Jay Mince collection.**

J. Muenzenberger and the *Truth*

About the Glenn Miller Sound

ONCE UPON A TIME, in the days when Frank Sinatra began crooning soft tunes for Tommy Dorsey, and Glenn Miller sat in the third row playing the trombone for Ray Noble, there emerged an immensely talented and happy clarinet player named John Henry Muenzenberger, who hailed from Chicago way and settled in Glen Head, Long Island. You know him as Johnny Mince. (Changed when a fan wrote to *Downbeat Magazine* saying he liked Benny Goodman, Artie Shaw, and that *other guy in Ray Noble's band.)* "Heck, I wasn't gonna take a chance on that happening again!"

Johnny was one of the Swing Era's sturdiest and most stellar players whose only goal in life was to play in a good band with the best musicians—and he has played with the best of them.

He began his career at the age of seventeen in New York with the Joe Haymes band which later became the Buddy Rogers band. Johnny's friend, Glenn Miller, who was managing the band for the Englishman, Ray Noble, signed him and Pee Wee Erwin into the organization after Buddy quit to join J. Arthur Rank in Hollywood and Noble took over. Glenn was also the band's arranger in those days. Players like Ziggy Elman, Buddy DeFranco, Davey Tough, Bunny Berigan, and Buddy Rich, along with arrangers Paul Weston, Axel Stordahl, and Sy Oliver were in the band. It was at the beginning of the Big Band Era and one of the best and most talented grass roots organizations.

Inadvertently Johnny became the catalyst for the original Glenn Miller sound. As we enjoyed a solid three hour lunch, at my friends Nelson and Monda Roberts Three Village Inn in old Stonybrook Village, one Tuesday afternoon in 1981, he told me the true story, and it differed from the silly Hollywood version portrayed in the *Glenn*

149

Miller Story where they show a trumpet player bumping his lip and then a clarinet player taking his spot in the band and thereby creating a reversal of instruments.

"The truth is that we were rehearsing with Ray Noble's band at the Rainbow Room on the 65th floor in Radio City. Trumpet player, Pee Wee Erwin called in sick, so Glenn asked me to play the trumpet part with the clarinet. 'I want to see what it sounds like,' said Glenn. He had been trying this 'sound' idea for years, but he didn't think to use the clarinet on top—playing a double with the tenor below. Pee Wee's playing had a wonderful high register that would play those very high notes with the saxophone voice underneath him. As it turned out, I don't think we went through the first eight bars and everyone knew that was the sound that Glenn Miller had been searching for all those years. It was written all over his face. That was the beginning of the famous Glenn Miller sound that punctuated his success as the most popular band of the era."

Still retaining traces of an early, mid-western drawl, John recounted another legendary tale: "One night up in that same Rainbow Room with Noble, before we got on the stand, several of us were warming up—Glenn comes up and says he had written a tune (a lesson composed for his teacher) and asked us to go over it. It was a beautiful thing and Glenn asked up to come down to Broadway the next day to record it. So we met in one of those studios on 49th street, and for just 25 cents recorded Glenn's immortal tune, *Moonlight Serenade*—little did we know...and I wonder what value that little plastic disc would hold today."

John was full of endless anecdotes about the Big Band glory days: "When Frank Sinatra was coming with the (Tommy Dorsey) band," he related vigorously, "we were ready to go on a one-nighter, and Tommy says, 'C'mere John."

He took me across the street and they had it on the juke-box—that thing he did with Harry James—*All Or Nothing At All*—yeah, that was it! I says, "Boy this guy is good!" his voice rising. "But my first impression meeting Frank, he was such a skinny, beat-up looking guy, compared to Jack Leonard (who was the singer who had just left the band) who had lots of class and was good-looking compared to Sinatra."

150

Johnny Mince about 1975. Jay Mince collection.

Johnny's association with Tommy Dorsey was another accidental fluke. He ran into Tommy on Broadway the day he returned from Chicago out of a job, and he says: "What are you doing in New York?" (the Buddy Rogers band had broken up a few days earlier in Chicago) and John told him what had happened. "Great!" says Dorsey, "you're taking Jimmy's (Dorsey) place tonight."

"Holy God!" John had said. "I'm taking my idol's place tonight."

John ran back to his hotel and gave his room mate a pair of new shoes for an extra tux he owned—and it didn't fit right—but he didn't care. He only knew he was playing in Tommy Dorsey's band that night. (He stayed on for six years until 1941.) He was a brilliant and most reliable member of the band, and contributed many well-structured fluent solos, adding a distinctive color to the band, the reed counterpart to Tommy's trombone. Get a copy of his 1938 version of *Chinatown, My Chinatown* and you'll see what I mean.

Unlike many players of his time, Johnny Mince did not become a leader, although he led small groups later on. "I had no ambition to become a bandleader. I was having too much fun. I ducked it!" He felt his freedom and a determination to become an excellent sideman was all the ambition he could handle.

Glenn and John were good friends, and when Glenn approached him about joining his newly formed band one night at Hurley's Bar, on Sixth Avenue at the foot of Rockefeller Center's NBC Studios, he and Pee Wee Erwin turned him down. "I didn't want to take a chance on being out of work again." He felt Glenn would have made a great leader and had everything going right for him, but he also knew Glenn had tried many times before to form a band and failed. (It was Woody Herman who told me that Glenn mortgaged his own and his in-laws home to finance previous attempts.) Glenn offered Johnny 50%, but he was earning $175.00 a week and did not want to jeopardize that. Today, those shares would have made him rich. Even after Glenn's plane disappeared in 1944 over the English Channel, the Glenn Miller Band has played almost uninterrupted for all these years right up to today, under its current leader, Larry O'Brien. (Just a few months ago Larry and the Band, with new singer, Frank Sinatra-like Tom Postilio, had just returned from an eight months European tour.)

Well, we rolled through one story after another, every one a gem. He recounted the legendary battles between Sinatra and Rich while they played with Dorsey, relating how Dorsey would physically restrain Sinatra, and he would hold back Rich after one of their confrontations. He revealed yarns about his twenty year stint (1946-66) with his mercurial boss, Arthur Godfrey, during both his radio and television days. (That followed an army discharge with five battlestars and a stint with Irving Berlin's *This is the Army Tour* for the U.S.O.)

In 1984, before heading South to retire in Florida, Johnny had been active with many jazz festivals including the Nice (France) festival with promoter George Wein, the Dick Gibson parties in Colorado, many Newport Jazz Festivals, the Sacramento, California festival, the Odessa and Midland Jazz Festivals in Texas, and, with time to spare, a short tour with Louis Armstrong. John's truly at his best when playing his beloved clarinet, although, like Woody Herman, he also played a mean sax. He was highly regarded as one of the best clarinet players of the swing era along with Benny Goodman, Woody Herman, and Artie Shaw, but never nearly as well-known. Maybe now you know him just a little bit better.

Trying to call Johnny at his Boca Raton, Florida, home for an update on his career, I sadly learned from his wife, Betty, that he passed from us in December of 1994. Fortunately, John's son, Jay, a popular educator on Long Island, was able to obtain photos of his dad for use in this book. The photos taken of us both by a bartender in the Sand Bar Room at The Three Village Inn were lost or misplaced. Anyway, I like these photos much better. It portrays Johnny Mince with his beloved instrument at two stages of his life.

The next time you hear a Glenn Miller recording, I hope you will now think of Johnny Mince, who helped give birth to that wonderful sound that distinguished itself during the Big Band Era.

Tom Postilio. Richard Grudens Collection.

Tom Postilio

New Kid on the Bandstand—Sinatra Style

*History repeats itself. There is nothing new under the sun. What goes around—comes around, a*nd lots of other clichés you have heard before. But this time we may have a *dyed-in-the wool* winner, (another cliché) and that's Tom Postilio, (like Sinatra—his real name) a vibrant young man singing music reserved for his parents and grandparents instead of the rock and roll of his own generation.

Tom is merely 25 years old but has already been featured at the fabled Village Gate and Eighty-Eight's and The Rainbow Room in Rockefeller Center, all in New York, New York (as the song says). He had a run at the prestigious Tavern on the Green in Central Park during the summer of '95, toured the world for 10 months with band leader, Long Island's own, Larry O'Brien and the Glenn Miller Orchestra, and performed to well over 16,000 people during one show alone featuring the Tommy Dorsey Orchestra with my friend Buddy Morrow and the Count Basie (with Frank Foster) Orchestras at the Hollywood Bowl. He opened for both the Phyllis Diller and Joan Rivers acts at Atlantic City's Harrahs Resort and made a perfectly classy sounding album of new and old standard gems entitled *What Matters Most* where he performs like a seasoned icon with poignant moments of brilliance. He seems best when the rhythms are upbeat and quick, as he did on an old Fred Astaire classic, *Slap That Base.* Very few sing songs like that nowadays.

"I couldn't imagine doing anything else. When I'm on stage I feel at home. I love what I do." Where have we heard that before? From Tony? Frank?

Backing up a little, Tom first fell in love with his Dad's archived Frank Sinatra albums when he was just a lad of thirteen. Sinatra inadvertently became his teacher and mentor. But that's only a few short

155

years ago. Some have told him not to emulate Old Blue Eyes, that it was a dangerous career road, but rather to find his own niche in both voice and delivery.

But, lest we forget, Frank Sinatra worshipped and mimicked Bing Crosby even to wearing a Crosby-style hat and smoking a Crosby-style pipe. And everybody copied everyone else. Tony Bennett, Frankie Laine, Perry Como, and Pat Boone all told me how they imitated Bing almost blatantly during the dawn of their own careers, and Tony Bennett admits to emulating Frankie Laine. Why, even Elvis mirrored Crosby and Dean Martin. So, is it so bad that Tom Postilio emulates Frank Sinatra? I think not.

Tom is completely committed to big band music. He's dedicated to the standards of Berlin, Porter, Rodgers and Hammerstein, and Jerome Kern. Meeting Tom is like meeting the young Sinatra. I found Tom to be charismatic like Sinatra, but much better looking and, although he sings like him, he really tries to avoid the label by selecting his own un-Sinatra songs. There was only one Sinatra recorded song in his album, *Let's Get Away From It All*.

"I really try hard not to choose selections that he is famous for...I really want my own audience. I don't want to be another Sinatra. I want to be *Tom Postilio* even though I can't help sounding a bit like him. We searched for seven months to find selections I could do that he hasn't. It was tough to find them. He has recorded so much."

That's the only way he'll beat the problem. During the long tour, Larry O'Brien said: "When he does Billy Joel numbers, he flatly sounds like Sinatra, especially with *Just the Way You Are,* he just can't help it."

Last summer, Tom and I sat down for a pasta dinner at my favorite restaurant, Sophie's, in St. James N.Y. where young host Greg Armine, who is Sophie's son, set us up in a perfect spot. We talked about everyone and anything for four hours and I learned a lot about this future star. (All the while Greg played Tom's new album on the restaurant sound system.)

At the age of 17 he won a talent competition sponsored by the Long Island newspaper *Newsday* and was showcased with others at the Harry Chapin Theater in Huntington, Long Island. It was the first thing done away from high school stage performances. He was

156

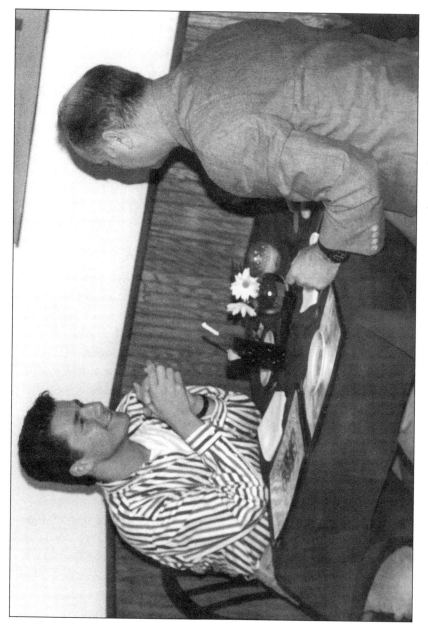

With young Tom Postilio at "Sophies." Photo by William DeBetta.

brought to the attention of local A.M. radio station WGSM by station copywriter Carol Grins, the mother of Tom's young schoolmate girl-friend at nearby Hauppauge High School. (Carol is now his tireless and enthusiastic publicist.)

Veteran disk jockey, Joe Roberts, my friend since the 1960's, played him frequently on-the-air and it was heard by agents for the Glenn Miller organization. Like his counterpart, Tom tries to surround himself with extremely talented personnel. He chose Rosemary Clooney's coveted John Otto to produce, arrange, and conduct his album, and selected the most impeccable musicians, writers and composers around to insure its success.

Five years from now, he says: "I'd like to be where my friend, Michael Feinstein, is today—fairly secure and accepted in this industry. I wouldn't complain if I became a Frank Sinatra-like status, but that's really pushing it to the highest."

"Do you really expect to make it *that* big?"

"Oh, absolutely, absolutely. In five years I will be closer to it. I've also come to the realization that it won't happen overnight...I used to be impatient and wanted everything to happen in two short years, and I've been at it for five and I see it starting to pick up and a momentum is going in the right direction and that's encouraging."

Tom credits brashy Harry Connick Jr. for the renewed public interest in big band music. Connick has certainly demonstrated that he can succeed and sell records. Of course he had a major label (CBS/Sony) blocking interference for him on the way to those winning touchdowns.

"He's not a romantic singer, but he is a good musician and singer, and is electrifying in his performances, that's for sure." Tom said.

So here's a confident, talented young performer who considers Sinatra his personal trainer, learns intonation from the sound of Barbra Streisand's voice, thinks Tommy LaSorda, Manager of the L.A. Dodgers was the nicest guy he ever met, and believes his Dad really taught him the *most*, and insists the song *Lush Life* is the one ballad he just can't master—but will keep on trying until he gets it right.

Tom Postilio is the new generation's antidote to the mostly incoherent Top 40 product played on most radio stations around. He is now one of a few young singers carrying the torch for the Big Band

Era. He travels far and wide. Tom keeps me regularly tuned in to his career by mail from far-flung stages and cruise ships ports. How far he goes is anybody's guess, for the road will be hard and long. My guess is that his enthusiasm and consistent hard work may help him keep all that wonderful music alive so our children may be able to enjoy it as we have over the last fifty years. As Tony Bennett once told me: "It's not *old* music, it's *good* music."

So, stay tuned. (Another cliché'?) Why not!

Willard Alexander

Big Band Salesman

In 1934, young Willard Alexander, a bright "band booker" who was working for MCA (Music Corporation of America) representing and promoting such popular sweet bands as Wayne King, Sammy Kaye, Horace Heidt, Guy Lombardo, and Eddy Duchin, crossed over to work for an equally large and aggressive talent agency called William Morris, (up 'til then a mostly vaudeville and nightclub star agency). There he initiated a big band department and developed a creative and efficient group handling such veterans as Duke Ellington, Paul Whiteman, and Count Basie, and bravely took on numerous new and untried avant-garde musical bands like those of Dizzy Gillespie, Billy Eckstine, and Charlie Spivak. He brought them to the attention of the public through strategic bookings in theaters, pavilions and night clubs all over the United States.

He stayed six years eventually forming his own, now legendary, Willard Alexander Agency Inc. of Madison Avenue (New York) with satellite offices in Chicago, Beverly Hills, and London, England. He represented the cream of the music industry.

I have concluded that Willard Alexander, known to be a tough business man, but also a very gentle and self-effacing man, a man with vision, and clearly a gentleman of the golden era, must somehow be held responsible for the success of many key players of the Big Band Era. It was in his junior year as a music major at the University of Pennsylvania, Willard first began his own agency business though he was merely a student. He formed a band whose success caused it to venture off campus to play dates along the Eastern Seaboard. He followed musicians and helped book and promote them wherever and whenever he could, so he got a really early start in what was to come.

161

One night in 1983 I ran into Willard Alexander backstage at Westbury Music Fair on Long Island where he had booked The Glenn
Miller Orchestra with Larry O'Brien as the then current leader. We
found ourselves on a two-man bench in the hallway listening to Dizzy
Gillespie relate funny stories, as he was always inclined to do at gatherings, and began our own intimate conversation.

"I guess you've been through this sort of thing a thousand times."
I said referring to the gathering in the hall just before showtime, the
noise almost drowning out our exchange of words.

"Well, quite a few over a period of many years...I guess that's
true. But, I always like to attend the opening night of a band run. It's
something I've always done." Willard had a bandage on his nose, having just returned from his doctor, the result of a minor operation earlier in the day. With the anesthesia wearing off, he was beginning to
feel a little bit uncomfortable and was being constantly interrupted by
well-wishers who somehow knew about his tender condition:

"Willard, I hope you don't mind me asking all these old and obvi-
ous questions."

"Oh, No! I'm always glad to talk about this wonderful business."

"How long have you been doing all this?"

"Well, I was an agent in business in Philadelphia even when I was
in college at the University of Pennsylvania where I was a junior. I
majored in music, studied music, and followed musicians. But then I
joined MCA which was a growing agency in 1934 and, of course, it
became the largest agency in the business. I was there for six years.
Then I resigned and founded the band department for the William
Morris Agency and then I soon opened my own agency which I still
have today...which is representation of many big bands....mostly."

It was actually a panacea of the Big Bands including Benny Goodman, Count Basie, Buddy Rich, Glenn Miller, Duke Ellington, Jimmy
Dorsey, Tommy Dorsey, Artie Shaw, and even Vaughn Monroe.

"Of course you know John Hammond well, but do you still get
together with him on talent hunts like the old days?"

"Sure, we get together occasionally, but he's not feeling too well
these days." He said. Actually it was Hammond who urged Willard to
fly out to Kansas City with him where they discovered Count Basie
who Hammond heard on the radio while traveling in a taxi.

With grand bandmaker Willard Alexander before Glenn Miller Concert, 1983.

Willard explained that Hammond was a wealthy young man who just liked music so he supported it and was always bringing new faces he thought were good and promoted them wherever and whenever he could. Billie Holliday and Benny Goodman were, also, discovered by Hammond. He introduced Willard to Benny and, after hearing Benny play, Willard booked him immediately on the "Let's Dance" radio program in 1935.

"He never was an agent or booker, he just got a kick out of it." Willard said. "You know Benny married his sister and they had two girls."

I liked Willard Alexander. He was really from the old school. A perfect gentleman from an earlier time, he wore a characteristic pin-striped, three-piece suit with a white oxford button-down shirt and a polka-dot tie. It was Willard who represented Benny Goodman at the time of the revolutionary 1938 Carnegie Hall Jazz Concert.

"Willard, that had to be quite a feat, you know, to get a popular *jazz* band to play one of the world's finest theaters where heretofore only serious classical music was performed."

The corridor noise was becoming so deafening that Willard began to shout his answers in my ears: "BELIEVE IT OR NOT, IT WAS VERY EASY TO MAKE BOOKINGS FOR THE JAZZ BANDS AT THAT TIME ALMOST ANYWHERE, THEY WERE BECOMING IN GREAT DEMAND AT ALL THE PAVILIONS."

"HOW DID YOU KNOW THE WORLD WAS READY FOR BENNY GOODMAN?"

"WELL, WE THOUGHT BENNY'S NAME WAS KNOWN WELL ENOUGH TO TRY IT. IT WAS A GUY NAMED WYNN NATHANSON, A PUBLIC RELATIONS MAN WHO WAS WORK-ING WITH BENNY ON THE CAMEL CARAVAN SHOW, WHO RECOMMENDED WE DO A CONCERT AT CARNEGIE HALL, BELIEVING THE WORLD WAS READY FOR BENNY'S KIND OF STUFF. YOU KNOW...IN THOSE DAYS THERE WERE VERY FEW CONCERT HALLS—NO AVERY FISHER OR LINCOLN CENTER..."

Then a hallway lull as several of the participants dispersed. Willard and I got up and ambled our way into a dressing room locat-ed a few feet across the corridor where Camille Smith, my photogra-pher, took a few photos.

"How did you work it all out?" I asked him as we arranged ourselves on a long leather couch where I had interviewed Billy Eckstine and Dizzy Gillespie earlier in the evening.

"Well, we all had something to do with it. We selected the services of Sol Hurok (the world-famous impresario). I did the actual booking and Hurok did the publicity...you know, getting out the word that modern jazz would be played at Carnegie Hall for the first time. It was the first Jazz concert Hurok had ever done. But his name carried weight in the field."

"And you were sure it would work?" I posed the question to him.

"Oh! Yes! When you get as big and as hot and confident as Goodman was in those days, why not? We felt we had a winner...and we were right. Filling 2,800 seats was no great thing for a concert hall. We were sure it would work. You know, it was a new approach...the beginning of great new things for the Big Bands."

"Would you say it was one of the great accomplishments of your life?"

"Well," he smiled thoughtfully, "I had a lot to do with it, not *all* to do with it, and Mr. Hurok had a *lot* to do with it...I kinda brought them together with Nathanson, but Benny was the key player because he could have done any concert anywhere at the time and I'm sure it would have succeeded. We certainly couldn't have done any better or been more successful. I guess I can say it was an important part of my career...Benny's too...and Hurok's...and even Nathanson's."

Willard wrote me in 1983 and requested a few of copies of the photos we took together that night: "Frankly," he wrote, "these are the best photos I've had in years. If possible, I would like to get the two of me alone and the one with the two of us. I'd like to have those in stock in the event I should get any requests."

"In the meantime, let's get together and have lunch soon. Thanks again."

My reply wrapped up this way: "Yes, let's get together and talk more music and history. I was really quite honored in your presence and thank you for talking to us and posing. Jazz owes a lot to you for your efforts, no one can ever deny that."

Willard passed on very shortly thereafter. He was 76. Another giant was gone.

WNEW 1130 news release

FOR IMMEDIATE RELEASE   CONTACT: Gloria Greene
212-986-7000

THE JOHNNY MERCER STORY
ON WNEW

New York, November 23rd - For our next Weekend Special, on Sunday, December 12th, WNEW will present "From Memphis to St. Joe, from New York to L.A.--the Johnny Mercer Story." It will be heard from 2-6PM.

Johnny Mercer, in addition to being perhaps the most prolific of all lyric writers (and four time Oscar winner), was also one of the leading record vocalists of the 1940's and, as an astute businessman, one of the three founders of Capitol Records and its guiding spirit in signing such artists as Nat Cole, Stan Kenton, Jo Stafford, Peggy Lee and Margaret Whiting, among others.

Miss Whiting and Ginger Mercer, Johnny's widow, will be among the guests. A portion of a Mercer interview and--by special arrangement with Maurice Levine--a Segment of Johnny Mercer at the Y (on the occasion of the salute at the YMHA during the Lyricists series) will be heard. Jim Lowe and William B. Williams will narrate.

WNEW is a Metromedia Station.

WNEW Blurb, mid 1980's. Richard Grudens Collection.

WNEW

The Melody Lingers On and On

Let me tell you about WNEW. This magical radio station took to the airwaves in 1934 and was, for me and millions of other New Yorkers, the flagship station for the Big Bands and the great vocalists for over 60 years. Disk jockey Martin Block's *Make Believe Ballroom* was the showcase for the bands, their sidemen, and vocalists spun on the "78" turntables daily from ten in the morning until two in the afternoon five days a week.

Block borrowed the show's name from Al Jarvis' similar program in Los Angeles. The format of the program never changed. Employing the notion of gentle fiction that each record was a live performance, Block welcomed popular bands and singers to an imaginary ballroom with a revolving stage. Each performer remained under a crystal chandelier for 15 minutes. Listeners visualized a ballroom in a theater of their own imagination.

On Friday nights Block previewed new releases. On Saturday it was the top twenty countdowns. He also showcased semi-annual popularity polls which carried weight with listeners, artists, and even record companies. The show could and did account for the success of many a recording, including Harry James' *You Made Me Love You* and many others, just by spinning them on the WNEW's turntables by Block and on programs like *The Milkman's Matinee,* an overnight disc jockey program.

The show seemed to create hit records, and all disc jockeys soon became the major promotion for the record industry. The show's theme song, *It's Make Believe Ballroom Time,* recorded by Glenn Miller, written by Harold Green, with lyrics by Martin Block and Mickey Stoner, remained its only theme even after the death of Glenn Miller in 1944.

What a joy it was to hear your favorite performer's recording get prime playing time on this station. You were always guaranteed that. WNEW commanded an astonishing 25% audience against strong network radio competition. Sponsors paid dearly for Martin Block's super salesmanship. For Big Band enthusiasts, the music of WNEW was a lifeline to the rest of the world.

In the late thirties, Block would broadcast a show called *Saturday Night In Harlem* and you could hear all the great black bands— Claude Hopkins, Maxine Sullivan, Duke, Count Basie, and Earl Hines. WNEW's live house band actually employed newcomers to short-term contracts as house singers, including Frank Sinatra, Dinah Shore, Bea Wain, and Helen Forrest. One night, Martin Block brought together Tommy Dorsey, Bunny Berigan, Roy Eldridge, Harry James, Coleman Hawkins, Gene Krupa, and Count Basie for a live session at the station. What a night that was!

At one point, in a legal suit, Fred Waring, Sammy Kaye, and Paul Whiteman sued WNEW to prevent them from playing records on the air, but lost the case in a landmark decision. At that time record labels carried the warning: *Not Licensed for Radio Broadcast.* The purpose was to prevent records from undermining performers contracts, which usually called for exclusive services. WNEW's victory opened the door for all radio stations to fill the air with recorded music. So we all owe a debt to WNEW.

After Block left the station, Jerry Marshall hosted the Ballroom, and then in 1944 William B. Williams joined the station and eventually took the helm of the Ballroom in 1958 where he stayed until his untimely death in 1986. His opening line would always be *Hello World.* It is safe to say that almost every jazz, big-band and popular vocalist of the period performed on or was interviewed live on WNEW one or more times, especially by William B. Williams (real name, William Breitbart from Babylon, Long Island) who would invite the performers up to the studio while he talked at length to them. Frank Sinatra was a regular confidant, ("He was my best friend," said Sinatra.) and it was Williams who coined the sobriquet, Chairman of the Board, alluding to Sinatra's position in the world of popular music.

WNEW's William B. Williams in his dressing room, 1985.

In 1958 the Big 10 Records Contest for recordings from 1935 to 1958 wound up as follows: *A Tisket, A Tasket,* Ella Fitzgerald; *I'll Never Smile Again,* Tommy Dorsey; *Begin the Beguine,* Artie Shaw; *Tenderly,* Rosemary Clooney; *In the Mood,* Glenn Miller; *Tennessee Waltz,* Patti Page; *White Christmas,* Bing Crosby; *My Blue Heaven,* Gene Austin; *Nature Boy,* Nat King Cole; *Sing, Sing, Sing,* Benny Goodman. What a lineup that was! Later, in the mid-eighties, a poll of the 50 best records of the previous 50 years included some of those same recordings with Bunny Berigan's *I Can't Get Started* as number one, *Begin the Beguine* as number 2, and *Sing, Sing, Sing,* as number three.

In the late seventies, the station turned to more contemporary music and Williams would be found spinning a *Meatloaf* or *Presley* record while on the telephone with Steve Lawrence and Eydie Gorme.

Then suddenly, the station reversed itself and moved to bring back The Make Believe Ballroom. With no advance announcement, The Ballroom returned one morning in 1979 at exactly 10 o'clock. "We wanted to find out if there was anybody out there." said Jim Lowe, program director. "The phone lines lit up. In five minutes we had jumped from Boz Skaggs to Ella Fitzgerald. Within a week, the entire station went right back to what it had been." Some kids wrote in to ask where they could reach Glenn Miller. Some of the station's old recordings were taken out of storage in Secaucus, New Jersey. Record companies supplied others, and some listeners actually brought in some out-of-print disks by such bandleaders as Hal Kemp and Vaughan Monroe.

The new term was: *Our Kind of Music,* meaning music in the WNEW formula. As Jim Lowe defined it; "The lovely songs written between 1935 and 1965." William B. was back playing the music he loved for the people who loved it. "Good music was back in business," according to Tony Bennett. It went over so well that an evening version of the *Make Believe Ballroom,* hosted by Bob Jones aired from six to eight every weekday night.

On December 2, 1992, WNEW left the airwaves. The station was losing money, so great jockeys like Bob Jones, Jonathon Schwartz, and Jim Lowe were silenced for a short while. Old New York radio Station WQXR was quickly converted from a long time classical music station to WQEW and our music was back on the air, same format, same enthusiasm, same personalities. Nobody was happier than singers like Margaret Whiting, Tony Bennett, Mel Torme, Kay Starr, and Lena Horne, who openly and often acknowledged their debt to the station. WNEW represented their life's career. WQEW was a timely heart transplant. The playing of good music on radio had returned to the airwaves triumphantly. The public demanded it. The public supports it.

It's Make Believe Ballroom Time,
Put All Your Cares Away.
All the Bands are here,
To Bring Good Cheer your Way.
Just close Your Eyes,
And visualize,
In Your Solitude,
Your favorite band is on the Stand,
And Mr. Miller puts you
In The Mood
It's Make Believe Ballroom Time,
The Hour of Sweet Romance
Here's Your Make Believe Ballroom
Come on, Children,
Let's Dance!
Let's Dance!

Warren Covington and the Pied Pipers.

With bandleader Warren Covington backstage at Westbury.

172

So All of Them Are My Favorites

Well, this compact book recounts just a handful of the facts and fables of the Big Band Era and a few seasons beyond. But, as Buddy Rich observed when continually surveyed about the possible organization of an all-star band and who, in his opinion, the great players would be: "...you can never form an all-star band simply because you cannot insult the other giants—so all of them are my favorites." Buddy admired all the stars and competitors of the era.

In retrospect, I wish I had begun earlier in my quest to personally meet and talk to more of my heroes about their contributions to the musical form. Nevertheless, I cannot close these chapters without some words of admiration for some of the others alluded to by Buddy...

WARREN and the Pied Pipers

Warren Covington was a capable trombone player in the Horace Heidt and Tommy Dorsey orchestras and later led his own band. When the *Reader's Digest* asked him to make an album with the Pied Pipers, the Tommy Dorsey vocal quartet of the forties where both Frank Sinatra and Jo Stafford honed their craft with romantic ballads and mood pieces, Warren went to the Dorsey estate and was surprised to discover that nobody owned the copyright to the name *The Pied Pipers*. "So I rushed to the Library of Congress and copyrighted and trademarked the name which I now own." he told me during an interview in 1985. During the eighties and right through today, Warren Covington features the Pipers in cruise ship and showcase performances and plays his trombone all over much like he did when he was a young man. The last time Warren Covington and I talked Big Band stuff from his Wyckoff, New Jersey home, he looked as though he was just 40 years old and living a great life.

Tommy Dorsey's Buddy Morrow and faithful friend.

And Grateful Thanks to

Charlie Barnet and *Cherokee;* Tex Beneke and *Chattanooga-Choo-Choo;* WNEW radio's 1991 poll winner of the Best Recording of the last 50 years, Bunny Berigan for *I Can't Get Started;* Les Brown, who has played so long for my friend, Bob Hope; and Doris Day, his vocalist of years past including her tremendous hit, *Sentimental Journey;* Frank Sinatra's swinging recording of *Sweet Lorraine* with jazz all-stars, Nat Cole on piano, Buddy Rich on drums, Coleman Hawkins on tenor sax, Johnny Hodges on alto sax, Charlie Shavers on trumpet, Ed Safranski on bass, and arranged by Sy Oliver. It's a perfect gem. A special thanks to Dick Sudhalter, journalist, writer, and cornetist who penned the vital story of an earlier cornet player, legendary Bix Beiderbecke, entitled, *Bix-Man and Legend.* My interview with him is not included here since he arrived on the musical scene well after the Big Band Era, but it's a great story nonetheless.

And how about Billy

With Glenn Miller bandleader Larry O'Brien.

175

Les Brown Band with vocalist Doris Day 1940 at the World's Fair. Photo credit: Ed Burke collection.

Butterfield's creamy trumpet rendition on Margaret Whiting's *Moonlight in Vermont;* Billie Holiday's own *God Bless the Child* recorded when she was *Lady Day, Queen of Jazz;* Cab Calloway rambling on *Minnie the Moocher;* perfectionist, Lee Castle, who is now leading the Jimmy Dorsey "ghost" band; Bing's brother Bob, who never played any instrument at all but led a great band; Xavier Cugat's latin classic, *My Shawl;* Jimmy Dorsey and his great vocalists Bob Eberly and Helen O'Connell who sang those wonderful duets, *Green Eyes, Tangerine, Amapola,* and *Brazil*; Maynard Ferguson and his great big band; Glen Gray and the original Casa Loma Orchestra (*Smoke Rings*); arranger, Jerry Gray, (he arranged Glenn's immortal *In the Mood*); Coleman Hawkins (who deserves a chapter of his own); Neal Hefti, (one of the best sidemen and arrangers ever); Fletcher Henderson's great work establishing the early Benny Goodman band; The sleek and smooth band of Artie Shaw (*Begin the Beguine, Frenesi*) and his courageous support of the hard-pressed, Billie Holiday; nutty Spike Jones and *Cocktails For Two;* the lovely and sleek Ina Ray Hutton, the only lady leader of the era; Stan Kenton and that stalwart powerhouse trumpet section; Kay Kyser and his crazy Kollege of Musical Knowledge; leader of the "sweetist band this side of heaven" Guy Lombardo and his Royal Canadians (*Auld Lang Syne*); and Jimmy Lunceford, one of the most influential pioneers of the twenties.

And how about the long list of premier artists who once performed with "Pops," King of Jazz Orchestra leader, Paul Whiteman, who featured all these wonderful guys and gals: genius cornetist, Bix Biederbecke (mentioned earlier); jazz-singer Mildred Bailey; song stylist, Billie Holiday; crooner, Bing Crosby, Roy Bargy and Frankie Trumbauer; jazz violinist, Joe Venuti; Jimmy and Tommy Dorsey, Jack and Charlie Teagarden, Henry (hot lips) Busse, arranger, Bill Challis, guitarist, (later backed Bing Crosby on many of his recordings and in the movies) Eddie Lang; and prolific composer and vocalist, Johnny Mercer. Whew!

And thanks too, Nat King Cole's trio and his golden rendition of *Route 66*; Clyde McCoy's trumpet on his *Sugar Blues;* Red Norvo, vocalist Mildred Bailey's band-leading husband; Tony Pastor, who helped launched the career of Rosemary Clooney; versatile "jazz-scat" singer Mel Torme, friend and biographer of drummer, Buddy Rich, who sang and played with the all of them. His book, *It Wasn't All Velvet* makes exemplary reading of that musical era.

Then there's Louis Prima and Keely Smith and their *Old Black Magic;* Chick Webb, who christened the career of the First Lady of Song, Ella Fitzgerald when she vocalized *A Ticket-A-Tasket;* Vaughan Monroe and his thrilling recording of *Ballerina;* The Dukes' classic, *Take the A Train;* Larry Clinton and Bea Wain's sweet rendition of *My Reverie,* Tommy Dorsey's trombone smoothing over *I'm Getting Sentimental Over You;* Ray McKinley—*You Came A Long Way From Missouri;* Alvino Ray and the King Sisters, Yvonne, Donna, Louise and Alyce. Ted Weems and his best-selling *Heartaches* underscored by Elmo Tanner's perfect whistling solo; Sammy Kaye's—*Do You Want to Lead A Band?* shows, and Yes!, Lawrence Welk's bubbles, and those cute little Lennon Sisters (whom we once interviewed—but, alas, they were a much later group); and the countless thousands of players, leaders, vocalists, arrangers, managers, and songwriters, who contributed invaluable services which helped create, cultivate, and harvest the great bounty known to us all as the Big Band Era.

Index

181

Westbury Music Fair, 44, 63, 73, 75, 121, 128, 14ɔ, 161, 172
Weston, Paul, 149
What Matters Most, album, 155
Wheel Of Fortune, 99, 101, 103
When I Take My Sugar to Tea, 28
When Johnny Comes Marching Home, 31
When Sunny Gets Blue, 47
When You Were Sweet Sixteen, 125
Where The Blue Of The Night Meets The Gold Of The Day, 85
Willard Alexander Agency, 161
White Christmas, 170
Whiteman, Paul, 2, 86, 89, 161, 168, 177
Whiting, Margaret, 4, 63, 64, 69-74, 103, 171, 177
Whiting, Richard, 71
Williams, Hank, 42

Williams, Joe, 50, 116
William Morris Agency, 161, 162
William B. Williams, 44, 62, 63-74, 123, 168-170
Wilson, John S.
Wilson, Teddy, 20, 21, 79, 114, 135-138
Woodchopper's Ball, 108
Wrap Your Troubles In Dreams, 88

Yes, My Darling Daughter, 31
Yesterdays, 21
You Came A Long Way From St. Louis, 178
You Made Me Love You, 5, 11, 167
Young, Trummy, 23
Your Cheatin' Heart, 42
Young, Gus, 105, 106, 136
Young, Lester, 50, 96

WITHDRAWN